SCOTT'S LAST VOYAGE

Edited by Ann Savours
Introduced by Sir Peter Scott

SCOTT'S LAST VOYAGE

Through the Antarctic Camera of Herbert Ponting

Sidgwick & Jackson

For John and Nicholas

Designed by Paul Watkins
First published in Great Britain in 1974
Copyright © 1974 Ann Savours
and Sidgwick and Jackson Limited

ISBN 0 283 98139 3

Filmset by Photoprint Plates Limited
Rayleigh, Essex
Printed by The Whitefriars Press Limited,
Tonbridge, Kent

for Sidgwick and Jackson Limited
1 Tavistock Chambers, Bloomsbury Way
London WC1A 2SG

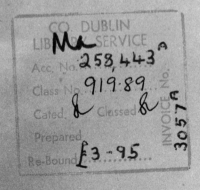

Introduction by Sir Peter Scott

Contents Antarctica 1910

Introduction by Sir Peter Scott

C.B.E., D.S.C.

On 17 January 1912 Captain Scott and his four companions, Wilson, Bowers, Oates, and Evans, reached the South Pole to find that they had been forestalled by the Norwegian explorer Åmundsen, who had been there one month earlier. My father and his party had 800 miles to walk back, hauling their sledge, to their base camp on McMurdo Sound. They died a hundred miles short of their destination. The diaries and letter found with their bodies in the following spring told a story that still fires the imagination of succeeding generations. The visual images which go with the story were provided by the drawings of Edward Wilson and the photographs of Herbert Ponting.

I was less than than two years old when the *Terra Nova* sailed to Antarctica and nearly three-and-a-half when the news of the disaster reached home. I grew up with the story and for me it was largely a 'picture-story'. The power of the picture-story began with the earliest cave paintings and runs all the way to television. For me perhaps the most important picture in the story is a large photograph by Ponting of my father writing at the table in his 'den' in the winter quarters hut at Cape Evans. It has been continuously on the wall

Photograph by Philippa Scott

of my various homes throughout my life. Pinned on the wall of the hut are snapshots of my mother and of me as a small baby.

In January 1966 I sat writing up my notes at the same spot in that hut. When one of my colleagues tried to photograph me he discovered that Ponting must have had an extremely 'wide-angle' lens to get so much of the back wall into the picture.

Five years later I was able to visit the hut again with my wife and eighteen-year-old daughter Dafila. I felt again the extraordinary aura of the place. The explorers might have left it six months before instead of sixty years. For most of the intervening time the hut was filled with powdered snow in which nothing decayed. The snow was carefully removed by a New Zealand team only a few years ago, and the New Zealanders still maintain this and the other historic huts in this sector of the Antarctic. The Cape Evans hut is perhaps the most beautifully situated of all, only twenty yards from the shore with the supreme backcloth of Mount Erebus, the still-smoking volcano. The hut itself, surrounded by snow-drifts, nestles most beautifully into the landscape, with the ice cliff of the Barne Glacier immediately to the north. Inside, cold though it is, it carries still a connotation of warmth and shelter. Only a few men have lived here, men who were happy, bored, hopeful and heart-broken, men whose adventures have become a part of history. We spent some time in the den—a kind of alcove from the main hut with my father's bunk along one wall and Wilson's bunk along the other. There was a stuffed Emperor Penguin on the table and a bound volume of the *Illustrated London News* with an article on 'The Kaiser as a Farmer'. Next to 'the den' came Ponting's dark room with lots of bottles and trays. It was from here, we read, that the tinkling sound of breaking glass often came when Ponting was destroying the plates which did not satisfy him.

Ponting was the official photographer, although he described himself as 'Camera Artist'. He was attached to the scientific staff of twelve, which made the expedition more directly orientated towards research than any previous polar expedition in history.

Ponting was both artist and brilliant technician. At one point my father wrote, 'He is an artist in love with his work.' Elsewhere he wrote, 'His results are wonderfully good, and if he is able to carry out the whole of his programme we shall have a photographic record which will be absolutely new in expeditionary work.'

6

Although the first beginnings of photography can be traced back to Niepce in 1822, and the successful experiments of Daguerre, Talbot and Herschel in the twenty years thereafter, it was not until about 1889 when Ponting was nineteen years old, that the photographic process was perfected. By the time of the *Terra Nova* expedition (and for a long time after that) photography was still regarded as some sort of extension of drawing and painting. It may be that the 'Camera Artists' have never become entirely emancipated. On the other hand photography wrought great changes in the history of painting, when the production of oil paintings which were 'the nearest thing to a coloured photograph' was found to be a limited artistic achievement. And this perhaps more than anything opened the road to abstract art.

Be that as it may, a Camera Artist who combined a highly discriminating eye for tone values and composition with an energetic enthusiasm for recording scenes that were altogether new, was clearly in a position to move people deeply, and Ponting did and still does so. What is that, if not art, for there was nothing fortuitous about his work?

Ponting was also among the very first movie cameramen, and again the quality is startlingly high when one sees the film today.

As you will read later in this book, Ponting's habit of persuading the expedition members to pose for his photographs gave rise to a new verb, to 'pont', which described the act of persuasion. Ponting's nickname was Ponko, and the *South Polar Times*—the periodical journal of the expedition which became enormously familiar to me as a small boy—carried some verses with a chorus which went to the tune of the Edwardian ditty 'Drink, puppy, drink':

'Pont, Ponko, pont and long may Ponko pont,
With his finger on the trigger of his gadget,
For whenever he's around, we're sure to hear
  the sound
Of his high speed cinematographic ratchet.'

When Ponko was not ponting or processing his plates or teaching his colleagues how to take photographs, he had an additional duty—to lecture to the party of thirty-three who were over wintering at the base camp on Cape Evans. For these lectures he used the slides he had taken in the many countries he had visited—Japan, China, India, and many more. My father recorded, after one of these, that 'Ponting would have been a great asset to our party if only on account of his lectures,

but his value as pictorial recorder of events becomes daily more apparent. No expedition has ever been illustrated so extensively and the only difficulty will be to select from the countless subjects that have been recorded by his camera.'

Well, the subjects were selected and published, and the photographs have become familiar to a vast number of people to whom the story of the expedition has come to have a special meaning. But not all the pictures were published or destroyed by Ponting himself as unsatisfactory. Now a number of new photographs, never previously published, appear in *Scott's Last Voyage—Through the Antarctic Camera of Herbert Ponting*.

I am delighted to be given this opportunity to be associated with the book and to pay homage to Herbert Ponting—Camera Artist.

Author's Acknowledgements

Some years ago, when I was a young member of staff at the Scott Polar Research Institute in Cambridge, an institution founded in memory of Captain Scott, I remember the Institute's first director, the late Professor Frank Debenham, who had been one of Scott's geologists, telling me how the evenings in the Hut, during the expedition, were often accompanied by the sounds of breaking glass. The noise was made by Herbert Ponting, the 'Camera Artist', who would never let any of his less successful photographic plates survive. It has been therefore a great pleasure to me to choose these examples of Ponting's work from the hundreds in the care of the Paul Popper Agency and to tell once again the story of those heroic days. The task also provided an occasion to work again at the Scott Polar Research Institute, to whose present director and staff I am indebted. I should like to thank particularly Dr C. W. M. Swithinbank, who identified the photograph of the camp at the Gateway; also Mr H. G. R. King, Mrs S. Gethin and Miss K. Hollick for their encouragement. I have also to acknowledge the kind permission of Miss Barbara Debenham to reproduce her late father's delightful account of 'Stareek'. Nothing would have been achieved without the forebearance of my husband and the support of Mrs A. Clare, Mrs C. Lewellin, Mrs S. Lewis, Mr and Mrs B. Merricks, Mrs D. M. Shirley and Mrs R. Wonfer.

Ann Savours
Little Bridge Place, March 1974

Antarctica 1910

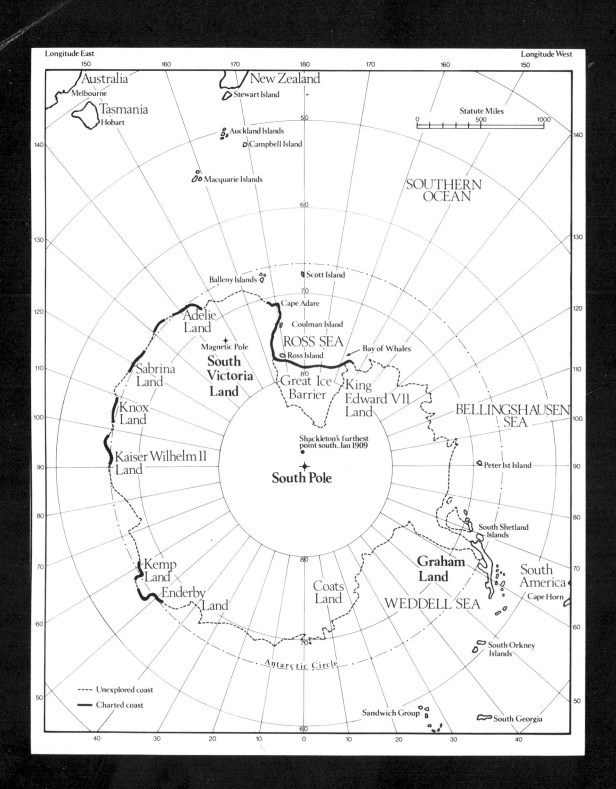

Longitude East   Longitude West

150   160   170   180   170   160   150

Australia

Melbourne

New Zealand

Stewart Island

Tasmania

Hobart

Statute Miles

0   500   1000

140

Auckland Islands

Campbell Island

SOUTHERN
OCEAN

140

Macquarie Islands

130

130

Balleny Islands

Scott Island

120

Cape Adare

Adelie
Land

Coulman Island

120

Magnetic Pole

ROSS SEA

Ross Island

Bay of Whales

Sabrina
Land

South
Victoria
Land

Great Ice
Barrier

King
Edward VII
Land

BELLINGSHAUSEN
SEA

110

Knox
Land

110

100

Peter Ist Island

100

Kaiser Wilhelm II
Land

Shackleton's furthest
point south. Jan 1909

90

South Pole

90

80

South Shetland
Islands

80

Kemp
Land

Graham
Land

South
America

70

Enderby
Land

Coats
Land

WEDDELL SEA

Cape Horn

70

60

South Orkney
Islands

60

Antarctic Circle

50

- - - Unexplored coast

Charted coast

50

Sandwich Group

South Georgia

40   30   20   10   0   10   20   30   40

The first two decades of the twentieth century have been called the 'heroic age' of Antarctic exploration—the time when men first ventured to sledge inland across the sea ice, the ice shelves, the glaciers and the ice sheets of the unknown seventh continent. Their struggles were tremendous and they themselves seem to have grown the greater as the contest proceeded against the power and treachery of the sea ice, the difficult surfaces of the snow, the biting winds and blizzards of ice shelf and ice sheet, the hidden crevasses of the glaciers and, on one occasion, against the darkness of the polar night.

Antarctica lies at the bottom of the world, isolated from the shores of South America, South Africa, Australia and New Zealand by the encircling and unbounded Southern Ocean. The continent consists mainly of ice, some of it several miles in depth, but there are mountain ranges of considerable extent and even an active volcano. During the Antarctic summer there is no night. During the Antarctic winter the sun sets and there is no day. In the autumn the sea freezes over; the young ice looks like fields of giant waterlilies. As temperatures drop and winter approaches, the sea ice thickens to form a highway strong and stable enough to bear men, dogs, machines and ponies. With the coming of the southern spring and the return of the sun, the sea ice begins to break up and it finally floats away.

For centuries maps and globes of the world had shown a great southern continent, marked *Terra Australis nondum cognita*, stretching across southern latitudes. The English navigator Captain James Cook whittled away much of this supposed land mass during his circumpolar voyage of 1772–75 in H.M. Ships *Resolution* and *Adventure*. Of the existence of the continent Cook wrote in his *Journal* on 21 February 1775, at the end of his circuit of the Southern Ocean: 'That there may be a Continent or large tract of land near the Pole, I will not deny, and it is probable that we have seen a part of it.' He goes on to describe the formation of the 'extraordinary islands of ice' (icebergs) and trusts that his description will 'convey some Idea of the Lands where they are formed, Lands doomed by nature to everlasting frigidness and never once to feel the warmth of the Sun's rays, whose horrible and savage aspect I have no words to describe.' Cook's work was complemented by a Russian expedition commanded by Captain Thaddeus Bellingshausen in the *Vostok* and *Mirny*, who deliberately went where Cook had not been, during a circumpolar voyage lasting from 1819 to 1821. Other exploratory voyages followed, some made by national expeditions, others by whaling firms and individual whalers and sealers. By the time Scott's first expedition, known as the British National Antarctic Expedition, 1901–4, set out from London in the *Discovery*, the maps of the Antarctic showed the continent as a great round iced cake, which had been nibbled at intervals along its edges. These coastal areas had been charted by men in wooden sailing ships, who landed, if it were possible to penetrate the sea ice, only to hoist a national flag or to look for seals.

With the end of the nineteenth century came the urge to explore inland and thus began the 'heroic age' of Antarctic exploration, the era of Scott, Shackleton, Amundsen and Mawson. All of them fought a relentless enemy and while reading and re-reading the published narratives of their expeditions, one may appreciate in some small measure their courage and foresight in success and their even greater endurance and resolution when defeated.

This book is concerned with one of these men—Captain Robert Falcon Scott, R.N., and his companions during the British Antarctic (*Terra Nova*) Expedition, 1910–13. Scott's Last Expedition, as it has become known, was the third of three British expeditions to winter on Ross Island, McMurdo Sound, in the early years of the twentieth century.

The Ross Sea, McMurdo Sound, Mounts Erebus and Terror and the Ross Ice Shelf were first discovered by Sir James Clark Ross, in command of the British Antarctic Expedition of 1839–43, in H.M. Ships *Erebus* (370 tons) and *Terror* (340 tons). These stout wooden sailing ships, known as 'bomb vessels', twice penetrated the pack ice which bounds the entrance to the Ross Sea. Ross's aim was to reach the South Magnetic Pole, as he had reached the North

Magnetic Pole ten years before. But his way was barred by the hundred foot high cliffs of the 'Great Ice Barrier' (now known as the Ross Ice Shelf), whose front he charted for over 400 miles. He made no explorations on foot of 'South Victoria Land', a desolate region of high mountains, great glaciers, ice sheets and blizzards, which he claimed as the first territorial acquisition of Queen Victoria's long reign.

Some sixty years later, a few months after the death of the Queen, the National Antarctic Expedition, commanded by Robert Falcon Scott, a young naval officer, left London in the *Discovery* to winter at Hut Point, McMurdo Sound. They made the first extensive land explorations of Antarctica and carried out a full scientific programme. Three years later, the British Antarctic expedition of 1907–9 in the *Nimrod*, led by Ernest Shackleton, built a hut at Cape Royds and from there made a tremendous journey to within ninety-seven miles of the South Pole. They too carried out a scientific programme, which included the location of the South Magnetic Pole.

Then followed the British Antarctic (*Terra Nova*) Expedition, 1910–13. In his preface to *Scott's last expedition*, Sir Clements Markham, President of the Royal Geographical Society, who had first set Scott on his path to the Pole by giving him command of the *Discovery*, wrote as follows regarding the aims of the *Terra Nova* expedition. 'The object of Captain Scott's second expedition was mainly scientific, to complete and extend his former work in all branches of science. It was his ambition that in his ship there should be the most completely equipped expedition for scientific purposes connected with the Polar regions, both as regards men and material, that ever left these shores. In this he succeeded. He had on board a fuller complement of geologists, one of them especially trained for the study of physiography, biologists, physicists, and surveyors than ever before composed the staff of a Polar expedition. Thus Captain Scott's objects were strictly scientific, including the completion and extension of his former discoveries . . . Never before, in the Polar regions, have meteorological,

magnetic and tidal observations been taken, in one locality, during five years. It was also part of Captain Scott's plan to reach the South Pole by a long and most arduous journey, but here again his intention was, if possible, to achieve scientific results on the way, especially hoping to discover fossils which would throw light on the former history of the great range of mountains which he had made known to science.'*

Captain Robert Falcon Scott was born in 1868 in the West Country, the elder son of six children, who lived a happy and adventurous childhood in the family home, 'Oatlands', Plymouth, a house with a garden, paddocks and outhouses. He entered the Royal Navy in 1886 as a cadet in the training ship *Britannia*. He became a Torpedo Lieutenant and served under various captains, including Captain Egerton of the *Majestic*, 1898–99. He was noticed by the eminent geographer, Sir Clements Markham, in 1887, when as a midshipman he won a Service cutter race. Sir Clements was in the earliest stages of forming an expedition to the Antarctic. He wrote of Scott, 'He was then eighteen and I was much struck by his intelligence, information and the charm of his manner. My experience taught me that it would be years before an expedition would be ready, and I believed that Scott was the man destined to command it.' In 1899, Scott met Sir Clements by chance in London, heard about the Antarctic expedition and two days later applied to command it. 'So it was that he set forth on a voyage of discovery, the aims of which were ostensibly geographical and scientific, but the inner purpose of which for him was the discovery of himself' (Seaver).

On the return of the *Discovery* to London from the Antarctic, Scott was promoted captain and was made a gold medallist of the Royal Geographical Society and similarly honoured by other learned societies and institutions. He wrote *The Voyage of the 'Discovery'*, which was published in 1905. He served in various ships of the Royal Navy, eventually securing a staff appointment at the Admiralty. In September 1908, he married Kathleen Bruce, the sculptor, who described their meeting at an Edwardian tea party in her autobiography *Self-portrait of an*

* In fact 35 lbs of geological specimens were sledged back from the Beardmore Glacier by the Pole party in 1912.

Artist: 'Then all of a sudden and I did not know how, I was sitting in a stiff, uncomfortable chair with an ill-balanced cup of tea, and being trivially chaffed by this very well dressed, rather ugly and celebrated explorer. He was standing over me. He was of medium height, with broad shoulders, very small waist and dull hair beginning to thin, but with a rare smile, and with eyes of quite unusually dark blue, almost purple . . . I had never seen their like.' Their brief years together were very happy ones. Their son, Peter Markham Scott, was born in 1909.

That same year Scott began organizing the *Terra Nova* expedition, determined to fulfil the promise of his first expedition to the Antarctic. Unlike the *Discovery* expedition, Scott's second expedition was not a national undertaking. As a result, one of his most difficult tasks was the raising of funds to pay for the ship, the food and supplies, clothing, scientific apparatus, dogs, tents, hut, ponies, sledges, motor sledges, wages and salaries. He lectured to the public on his plans and contacted officials, businessmen and schools not only in many cities and towns of the British Isles, but also *en route* in South Africa, Australia and New Zealand. Despite Sir Clements' assertion that Scott's aims were largely scientific, the conquest of the South Pole for the British Empire was one of the mainsprings of his pleas for money. In the early pages of E. R. G. R. Evans's *South with Scott* and in the other narratives, one may read of the preparations for the expedition, of the appointment of staff and of the fitting out of the *Terra Nova* (744 tons). This Dundee whaler was built in 1884 by Alexander Stephen and Sons. She had been one of the two relief ships for Scott's *Discovery* expedition, whose arrival with the *Morning* in McMurdo Sound on 5 January 1904 was such a surprise at the time for Scott. To reach the Antarctic quickly, she had been towed half-way across the world on Admiralty orders, by cruiser after cruiser, at a speed which 'must have surprised the barnacles on her stout wooden sides' (Scott).

One of Scott's first acts after setting up an office for the British Antarctic Expedition in Victoria Street, London, in September 1909, was to send a wire to one of the former members of the *Discovery* expedition, Dr Edward Adrian Wilson, who had served as second surgeon, artist and vertebrate zoologist in 1901–4, requesting him to organize and lead the scientific staff of the new expedition. This Wilson agreed to do, despite tremendous pressure of other work. Edward Adrian Wilson was one of the finest and staunchest men that any expedition could wish to number among its members. His watercolours of the Antarctic (now mostly in the Scott Polar Research Institute, Cambridge) are superb. His observations and results as a scientist were first class and as a man he ranked 'very high in the scale of human beings' (Scott). His integrity, his sense of duty, his care for others, his quiet humour and his disregard for himself sprang from his Christian faith.

The photographer of the expedition was Herbert George Ponting, who was born in Salisbury in 1870 and who died in London in 1935. He travelled in many parts of the world during the first half of his life—first buying a ranch in California and then taking up

photography professionally in 1900. He went on a tour of the Far East in 1901, thus beginning a decade of globe-trotting. He was a correspondent during the Russo-Japanese War, 1904–5; he was in China and India during 1906–7 and back in Europe, taking photographs of mountains in France and Switzerland, in 1908. He also visited Korea, Manchuria, Spain, Portugal, Russia, Java and Burma. His photographs and articles appeared in many journals and periodicals, including *Harper's, Strand, Pearson's, Illustrated London News* and the *Graphic*. He wrote two books: *In Lotus-land Japan* (London 1910) and *The Great White South* (London, 1921). They were both successful, the first warranting a second edition in 1922 and the *Great White South* being reprinted as recently as 1950. He made a film during the Antarctic expedition, first shown in various forms and remade in 1933 as 'Ninety Degrees South', but although his reputation was much enhanced by his Antarctic work, the results brought him little financial reward. The latter part of his life is a sad record of business ventures, few of which were successful. For a more detailed account of his life and work, see H. J. P. Arnold's *Photographer of the World* (London, 1969).

Captain Scott much appreciated Ponting's work. In April 1911, he wrote: 'Of the many admirable points in this work, perhaps the most notable are Ponting's eye for a picture and the mastery he has acquired of ice subjects; the composition of most of his pictures is extraordinarily good, he seems to know by instinct the exact value of foreground and middle distance and of the introduction of "life", whilst with more technical skill in the manipulation of screens and exposures, he emphasises the subtle shadows of the snow and reproduces its wondrously transparent texture. He is an artist in love with his work and it was good to hear his enthusiasm for results of the past and plans for the future.' Ponting gives a certain amount of information in his Antarctic book about the technical side of his work. He was a very serious and dedicated professional artist—a fact not always appreciated by his fellow expedition members, to whom so often

he must have appeared as an onlooker or recorder and not a participant. They pulled his leg, however (as nearly everyone's leg was pulled), about the 'evil eye' of his camera, as he explains in *The Great White South*, pages 180–81: 'This was the third mishap that had occurred when I was photographing—first Gran's fall when ski-ing; then Clissold's fall from the iceberg, and now Debenham was *hors de combat*. Also, I had had several narrow escapes myself, since my adventure with the Killer whales. The whale incident had, of course, inspired numerous quips about Jonah; and Taylor had invented a new verb, consisting of the first syllable of my name—"to pont", meaning "to pose, until nearly frozen, in all sorts of uncomfortable positions" for my photographs. This latest mishap revived all the former quizzing about the evil eye propensities of my camera, and I was once again the butt for no end of twitting about "the peril of 'ponting' for Ponko"—the latter being my nickname. The more I protested—that I had kinematographed Gran's feat at his own special request; that I had taken every possible precaution to ensure safety when out with Clissold; that Debenham had fallen twenty minutes after I had taken my film, and instanced the scores of occasions on which nothing had occurred to mar the success of my pictures—the more persistently these crimes were fastened on to me.

'But such railleries were always good-natured, and everyone in the Hut was subjected to them whenever the slightest occasion presented. No opportunity was missed of poking fun at one another, and everyone hastened to give as good as he received whenever he had a chance of "getting his own back". The saving grace of humour served us in good stead always.'

Ponting taught photography to Debenham, Wright, Taylor, Bowers and Scott (his account of Scott's apprenticeship is amusing and revealing of Scott's character).

His work as a black-and-white photographer in the Antarctic still stands supreme—only equalled perhaps by Frank Hurley during Shackleton's *Endurance* expedition, 1914–16.

When Ponting died, Cherry-Garrard wrote of him, 'He came to do a job, did it and did it well. Here in these pictures is beauty linked to tragedy—one of the great tragedies—and the beauty is inconceivable for it is endless and runs to eternity.'

The poem quoted below was contributed by Meares to the *South Polar Times*, the expedition's newspaper-cum-journal, edited by Cherry-Garrard:

Pont, Ponko, Pont

I'll sing a little song, about one among our throng,
Whose skill in making pictures is not wanting.
He takes pictures while you wait, 'prices strictly
*   moderate';*
I refer, of course, to our Professor Ponting.

(Chorus)
Then pont, Ponko, pont, and long may Ponko
*   pont;*
With his finger on the trigger of his 'gadget'.
For whenever he's around, we're sure to hear the
*   sound*
Of his high-speed cinematographic ratchet.

When he started in the ship he was d——ly sick,
And couldn't make a picture for a day or two;
But when he got about, we began to hear him
*   shout,*
'Please stand still for a moment while I take you.'

When at last we reached the ice, he landed in a
*   trice,*
And hurried off to photograph the whales O!
But the 'killers' heard the sound, and quickly
*   turned around,*
And nearly made a meal of poor old Ponko.

In the dreary winter night he fixed up his carbide
*   light,*
And took us round the world as quick as winkin'.
And his spicy little yarns, about foreign countries'
*   charms,*
Were as good as any published in the 'Pink Un'.

Then pont, Ponko, pont, and long may Ponko
*   pont;*
With his finger on the trigger of his 'gadget'.
For whenever he's around, we're sure to hear the
*   sound*
Of his high-speed cinematographic ratchet.

It is perhaps fitting to end this introductory chapter with some brief notes on the other members of the expedition who appear in this book:

Lieutenant H. R. Bowers, Royal Indian Marine, known as 'Birdie' because of his beaky nose, was born in 1883. He was a cadet in the *Worcester* and sailed to Australia in a sailing barque, while serving his indentures as midshipman R.N.R. He was stationed in Burma and Ceylon from 1905 to 1910. Through his interest in the *Discovery* and *Nimrod* expeditions to the Antarctic, he met Sir Clements Markham, who introduced him to Scott. He

was a very tough traveller and an excellent organizer of the stores.

Lieutenant Wilfred M. Bruce, R.N.R., was born in 1874 and died in 1953. He joined the expedition in June 1910 and travelled to Vladivostok to help Meares with the ponies and dogs. He served in the ship's party throughout the expedition. He was Scott's brother-in-law.

Apsley Cherry-Garrard, known as 'Cherry', was assistant zoologist and editor of the expedition's newspaper *The South Polar Times*. He was born in 1886 and died in 1959. He wrote *The Worst Journey in the World*, first published in 1922, a work of great literary merit.

Frank Debenham, known as 'Deb', was one of the two Australian geologists of the expedition. He was born in 1883 and died in 1965. In 1920, he founded the Scott Polar Research Institute and was its first director. He later became the first professor of geography at Cambridge.

Lieutenant E. R. G. R. Evans, R. N., (later Lord Mountevans) known as 'Teddy', was born in 1881 and died in 1957. He joined the Royal Navy in 1896 and as sub-lieutenant in the *Morning*, took part in the relief of Scott's *Discovery* expedition in 1902. He joined the *Terra Nova* in 1910, as navigator and second-in-command. He was leader of the last supporting party to leave Scott on the Pole journey and survived the journey back to base through the exertions of his companions and subordinates Lashly and Crean. He was invalided home suffering from scurvy in 1912, but returned to the Antarctic in the *Terra Nova* in command of the final relief expedition. During the First World War, he became known as 'Evans of the *Broke.'* His book *South with Scott* was first published in 1921.

Petty Officer Edgar Evans, R.N., known as 'Taff' or Seaman Evans. He was born in 1876 at Rhossili, South Wales and joined the Royal Navy in 1891. He served in Scott's *Discovery* expedition, 1901–4. He was known as the 'strong man' of the *Terra Nova* expedition and a great worker.

Sub-Lieutenant Tryggve Gran, Norwegian Naval Reserve, was the ski expert. He was born in 1889 in Norway and was educated there and in Switzerland. He met Scott in Norway in March 1910 through Fridtjof Nansen, while Scott was testing one of the motor sledges. He demonstrated his ski-ing techniques and Scott at once enlisted him for the expedition to teach the use of skis to others. He was one of the party to find Scott's tent in November 1912. He served in the Norwegian Flying Corps and in the Royal Flying Corps during the First World War. He later rejoined the Norwegian Air Force and was a prisoner-of-war after the fall of Norway. He is now retired at Grimstad, Norway.

Cecil Meares was in charge of the dogs. He had travelled in many out-of-the-way parts of the world. He was responsible for obtaining the dogs from the lower Amur River region in Siberia, where he met the dog driver Demetri Gerof, whom he recruited to join the expedition.

Captain L. E. G. Oates, Inniskilling Dragoons, known as 'Titus' or 'The Soldier', was born in 1880. He had served as a subaltern during the Boer War and later served in Egypt and India. As an officer of a cavalry regiment, he knew horses well and took care of the ponies of the expedition, some of whom were very difficult customers. His assistant was Anton Omelchenko, who joined the expedition after meeting Wilfred Bruce, Scott's agent in Vladivostok. The famous painting entitled 'A very gallant gentleman' of Oates going out to meet his death in the blizzard, hangs in the Cavalry Club, London.

G. C. Simpson, known as 'Sunny Jim', was the meteorologist. He was born in 1878 and died in 1965. He was educated at Owens College, Manchester, then worked in the Meteorological Office, before joining the Indian Meteorological Service in Simla in 1906. He later became Director of the Meteorological Office, London.

T. Griffith Taylor, known as 'Griff', was one of the two Australian geologists of the expedition. He was born in 1880 and died in 1964. His narrative of the expedition *With Scott: the silver lining* was published in 1915. He later enjoyed a distinguished academic career in the geography departments of the universities of Sydney, Chicago and Toronto.

C. S. Wright, known as 'Silas', was the physicist of the expedition. He was born in 1887 in Toronto and was educated in Canada and in Cambridge. He served with distinction during the First World War. He later directed the Admiralty Research Laboratory, then became Director of Scientific Research at the Admiralty and finally head of the Royal Naval Scientific Service. He returned to North America to continue his own research and is now retired near Vancouver.

1 The Voyage South

Previous pages: Evening in the pack, 9 December
1910
Below: The *Terra Nova* in heavy weather

The Ross Sea is an extensive bight in the coast
of Antarctica some 1,500 miles almost due south
of New Zealand. A ship bound there must cross
twenty degrees of latitude—the fifties and
sixties south—and must be able to withstand
the cold and tempestuous weather of the
Southern Ocean. The *Antarctic Pilot* tells us,
'It is an exceptional month in which, at any
point between 50° S and Antarctica, there are
not several days of gale, and an exceptional
year in which there are not one or more days
with wind reaching Beaufort force 12.' The
Pilot goes on to say, 'The shores of the
Antarctic continent are surrounded by a medley
of floating ice, comprising bergs and pack-ice,
extending northward to varying distances,
forming an ice field, the forcing of which may
be attended with great difficulty and danger to
ships endeavouring to make the continent.'
Scott had beginner's luck during his first
voyage to the Antarctic in the *Discovery*. He was
spared a gale and he took only four days to get
through the pack-ice and into the open water of
the Ross Sea. This time he was not so lucky.

The *Terra Nova* left Lyttelton, New Zealand,
on 25 November 1910 and was seen off by a
great crowd of people. She was deeply laden
with three motor sledges, prefabricated huts,
provisions and gear for the expedition in the
Antarctic and with 464 tons of coal, boatswain's
stores, wire hawsers, canvas for sail-making,
carpenter's stores, cabin and domestic gear for
the ship. There were, too, the engineer's stores,
a blacksmith's outfit, fireworks for signalling,
whale boats and whaling gear, flags, logs, paint
and tar, a library of polar literature and another
library in miniature.

The steamship *Terra Nova*, largest and
strongest of the old Scottish whalers, had been
considerably altered for her role as expedition
ship. She was re-rigged as a barque. An
ice-house for mutton carcases was constructed,
her galley was almost rebuilt and a new stove
was put in. The forecastle was fitted up with
mess tables and lockers, while a lamp room (for
paraffin lamps), store rooms, instrument room
and chronometer room were added. The saloon
was enlarged to accommodate twenty-four
officers. Stables were erected under the

forecastle for fifteen of the ponies, while the other four were tethered to leeward of the fore-hatch under tarpaulins. The thirty-three sledge dogs were chained to stanchions, rails and ring-bolts. Pet rabbits lolloped about—'a floating farmyard best describes the appearance of the upper deck', wrote E. R. G. R. Evans in *South with Scott*.

Captain Scott, in his diary entry for 1 December 1910, writes of the ponies. 'Under the forecastle fifteen ponies close side by side . . . swaying, swaying continually to the plunging irregular motion. One takes a look through a hole in the bulkhead and sees a row of heads with sad, patient eyes come swinging up together from the starboard side, whilst those on the port swing back; then up come the port heads, whilst the starboard recede.' The ponies were well cared for by Captain L. E. G. Oates and by their Russian groom Anton Omelchenko. Scott continues by describing the unpleasant situation of the dogs. 'Upon the coal sacks, upon and between the motor sledges and upon the ice-house are grouped the dogs, thirty-three in all. They must perforce be chained up and they are given what shelter is afforded on deck, but their position is not enviable. The seas continually break on the weather bulwarks . . . The dogs sit with their tails to this invading water, their coats wet and dripping. It is a pathetic attitude, deeply significant of cold and misery; occasionally some poor beast emits a long pathetic whine.'

Many of the humans felt equally miserable with seasickness. Ponting 'cannot face meals but sticks to his work' wrote Scott; also on 1 December, 'Yesterday he was developing plates with the developing dish in one hand and an ordinary basin in the other.' Things were made almost unbearable by a violent gale the next day. Huge waves washed over the ship setting the loose coal-bags in motion on deck, where they acted like battering-rams. Some ten tons of precious coal, intended for the cruising programme, had to be thrown overboard. Nearly all hands were occupied in the waist of the ship. Oates and Atkinson laboured with the ponies the entire night. Two of them died. Meares and helpers had constantly to be rescuing the dogs. One drowned.

About 4 a.m. the engine-room reported that the pumps had choked and that the water was gaining despite all efforts. A human chain was started and by continuous baling with buckets, the water in the stoke-hold was kept under. Dr Edward Wilson, Chief of Scientific Staff, described the scene in his diary. 'It was a weird night's work with the howling gale and the darkness and the immense sea running over the ship every few minutes, and no engines and no sail, and we all in the engine-room black as ink with engine-room oil and bilge water, singing shanties as we passed up slopping buckets full of bilge, each man above slopping a little over the heads of all of us below him, wet through to the skin . . . and the rush of the wave backwards and forwards at the bottom grew hourly less in the dim light of a couple of engine-room oil lamps whose light just made the darkness visible.' They worked in two shifts, two hours on and two hours off all Friday and Friday night, while all the time the ship rolled 'like a sodden lifeless log, her lee gunwale under water every time.' Eventually the suction valve of the hand pump was reached and cleared of coal balls. Next morning the main hand pump was manned and by 12.30 the excess water was cleared. The swell continued to subside, making everyone very cheerful. The colder weather made people hungry and Scott noted with a slight tremor the amount of food needed to appease twenty-four young appetites in the saloon.

En route for the Antarctic

Previous pages: On deck with the dogs

Below: Captain Scott (on left with pipe) and others relaxing in the sun. Right: Dr Adrian Wilson (wearing balaclava) and Commander Harry L. L. Pennell, R.N., salting seal skins for preservation as zoological specimens. Far right: Dennis G. Lillie (on left), Biologist in Ship, and G. Murray Levick, Surgeon, R.N., examining a trawl catch, 24 January 1911. Bottom right: Lieutenant Henry E. de P. Rennick, R.N., and the sounding machine

Following pages: Captain L. E. G. Oates, Inniskilling Dragoons, who was in charge of the ponies during the expedition

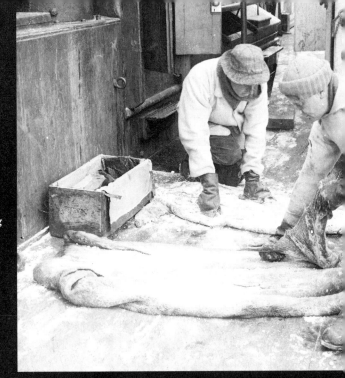

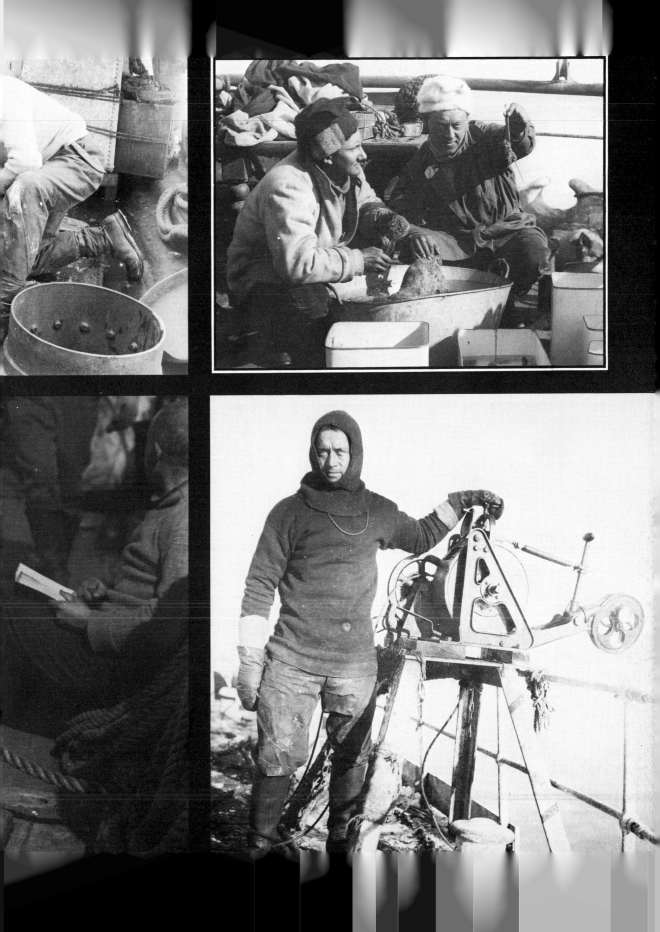

The first icebergs and pack-ice were reported on the morning of 9 December in latitude 65° 8′ S, further north than expected. The ship made slow progress south by dint of a continuous fight with the pack-ice. The Norwegian ski-runner Tryggve Gran took the opportunity to instruct the men of the landing party in the use of skis. The dogs were taken over the side by Meares for a sledge run. Wilson wrote on Sunday, 11 December 1910, 'We are now within the Antarctic Circle. The sunlight at midnight in the pack is perfectly wonderful. One looks out upon endless fields of broken ice, all violet and purple in the low shadows, and all gold and orange and rose-red

on the broken edges which catch the light, while the sky is emerald green and salmon pink, and these two beautiful tints are reflected in the pools of absolutely still water, which here and there lie between the ice floes. Now and again one hears a penguin cry out in the stillness near at hand or far away, and then, perhaps, he appears in his dress tail coat and white waistcoat suddenly upon an ice floe from the water—and catching sight of the ship runs curiously towards her, crying out in his amazement as he comes, from time to time, but only intensifying the wonderful stillness and beauty of the whole fairy-like scene as the golden glaring sun in the south just touches the horizon and begins again

The first pack ice in lat. 65°8′S on 9 December 1910, looking aft

behaved splendidly', wrote Scott, '—no other ship, not even the *Discovery* would have come through so well . . . As a result, I have become strangely attached to the *Terra Nova*. As she bumped the floes with mighty shocks, crushing and grinding a way through some, twisting and turning to avoid others, she seemed like a living thing fighting a great fight.'

The ship made a very unusual quantity of water, which in the end was traced to a badly fitting bolt in her timbers, underneath the iron sheathing of her forefoot. Since the steam-pump used up much precious coal, it was necessary for the man-pump to be frequently operated. Ponting describes the manning of the crank in *The Great White South*: 'Twice, daily, and once in the night watches, sixteen of the ship's company, officers and men together, would man this crank, and to the lively shanty, "Ranzo, boys, Ranzo", a flood of water pumped from the lip of the pump, until the soloist reached the stanza reciting the hero's promotion to the command of the ship, about which time chuckling and gurgling sounds emerging from the well and the easy swing of the great cranks indicated that the valves were sucking air and that the bilge was once more normal.'

Ponting also describes the taking of soundings in the pack-ice—a gruelling task for a number of hands working a small winch in ten-minute shifts. He writes of the work of Lillie and Nelson, the biologists, with their tow-nets, which trapped many small sea creatures and minute organisms. The catches were sorted and selected specimens were examined under the microscope. Others were preserved in glass jars for examination at home. 'To peep through the eye of our biologists' microscope at the details of their catch, was to enter such a world as bewilders description. Seen through this magic medium, organisms so diminutive as to be almost invisible to the unaided sight assumed a girth of inches; less minute organic forms became ferocious beasts; and tiny crustaceans, a millimetre long, became such monsters as one almost shrank from, with evil eyes and voracious-looking jaws.' Other studies were made of whales, seals, penguins, birds and fishes, sea ice and icebergs, sea temperatures and magnetism.

to gradually rise without having really set at all.' Wilson sketched and Ponting took some beautiful photographs. Scott grew anxious at the *Terra Nova's* consumption of coal, while trying to push through the pack and avoid icebergs. He remarked with pleasure 'the steady progress that proceeds unconsciously in cementing the happy relationship that exists between the members of the party'. Christmas Day, imprisoned in the pack, was celebrated with penguin instead of turkey and a five-hour sing-song. The *Terra Nova* was released after twenty days in the pack on 30 December 1910 and entered the open waters of the Ross Sea, having expended 61 tons of coal. 'The ship

The *Terra Nova* sailing through the pack ice,
11 December

Above: Pack ice and penguins, 28 December and
(right) working the pram through the pack
to reach a group of penguins

PONTING'S COLOUR PHOTOGRAPHS

Fascinating examples of early colour photography

In 1904 Auguste and Louis Lumière developed a colour process known as Autochrome which Ponting was to use in his work in the Antarctic. In 1907 the first plates were produced for sale at the Lumière plate-making factory at Lyons. These were to be the first colour plates to enjoy some measure of commercial success.

Tiny transparent starch grains were dyed red, green and blue, mixed, and then evenly sprinkled on to the glass plate which was coated with a sticky substance. The grains were then rolled, any white spaces left being filled with carbon black. Then the surface was covered with a panchromatic emulsion.

The plate was exposed with the glass facing the lens so that the dyed grains acted as a colour filter to the emulsion. After one development it was re-exposed to the light, then re-developed. The result was a transparency composed of small specks of primary colours— clearly visible through a magnifying glass—

giving a total effect of a coloured image.

Ponting was to take several colour pictures of varying quality, the best ones being those taken from Camp Evans which showed the afterglow in autumn, two of which are reproduced here. In *The Great White South* he wrote, 'Messrs Lumière & Co. of Lyons have presented me with a number of boxes of Autochrome plates for photographing in natural colours, though they did not hold out much hope that the plates would retain their qualities for more than a few months. The plates were really too old to obtain satisfactory results by the time I had an opportunity of using them on the beautiful afterglow effects we had in the autumn, and they had deteriorated in the slow journey through the heat of the Tropics. But though the cloud formations were unfortunately nondescript, I secured some very interesting records of afterglow with these plates.'

Below: Sunset, 10 April 1911
Right: Afterglow at 6 p.m. on 1 April 1911
(30 secs F11)

Below: Afterglow at 6.15 p.m. the previous day

Opposite: The *Terra Nova* held up in the pack, 13
December 1910
Following pages: The pack at Christmas Eve, 1910

2 The Landing at Cape Evans

Previous pages: North Beach, hut and Mount
Erebus from the west, 7 March 1911

Below: An iceberg breaking away at Cape Crozier,
3 January

Both Captain Scott and Dr Wilson had made the voyage to the Ross Sea and McMurdo Sound before, during the British National Antarctic Expedition of 1901–4 in the *Discovery*, Scott's first expedition. They had hoped that winter-quarters for the *Terra Nova* expedition could have been set up at Cape Crozier, where the 'Great Ice Barrier' (now known as the Ross Ice Shelf) joins the land and where the Emperor penguin breeds. 'Reluctantly and sadly', wrote Scott on 3 January 1911, 'we have had to abandon our cherished plan—it is a thousand pities. Every detail of the shore promised well for a wintering party. Comfortable quarters for the hut, ice for water, snow for the animals, good slopes for ski-ing, vast tracks of rock for walks. Proximity to the Barrier and to the rookeries of two types of penguins—easy ascent of Mount Terror—good ground for biological work—good peaks for observation of all sorts—fairly easy approach to the Southern Road, with no chance of being cut off—and so forth. It is a thousand pities to abandon such a spot.' A boat inspection had revealed that it would be quite impossible to land the stores, ponies, huts and other items owing to the lack of a sheltered beach and the considerable swell. Ponting too was extremely disappointed that day. Captain Scott had spoken enthusiastically to him in London of the 'Great Ice Barrier', that eighth wonder of the world, and it had been arranged that the ship should steam along the icy cliffs for several miles, while photographs and moving pictures were obtained. But the long delay in the pack forced Scott to abandon the project, much to Ponting's chagrin, as he watched the 'bastioned rampart' slowly disappear astern.

The *Terra Nova* rounded the tip of Ross Island and entered McMurdo Sound, familiar to several of the expedition from *Discovery* days. It was decided that winter-quarters should be established at Cape Evans, where the ship could be made fast with ice anchors to the hard icefoot. There were several other advantages to the site. A hard week's work began—disembarking and assembling the hut, landing the stores, pony fodder, fuel, scientific apparatus, provisions and furniture.

Below: The *Terra Nova* and a berg at the icefoot, 16 January 1911, and a view from a cavern in a stranded iceberg (left), 8 January

Ice reflections, with the *Terra Nova* in the distance,
7 January 1911

The ponies enjoyed a roll on the ice and
became quite lively, despite their sufferings
during the voyage. They pulled hard, bringing
ashore loads of between 700 and 1,000 pounds.
Meares and Demetri worked the dogs with light
sledge loads, but found great difficulty in
stopping the dogs from chasing and eating
penguins.

Two of the motor sledges did useful work in
transporting stores across the ice to the rocky
shore. But the third was lost when it sank
through the ice on to the sea bed, before ever
reaching land. This was a great blow to Scott,
who had high hopes of mechanized transport in
the Antarctic. Those members of the expedition
not helping in other ways, formed themselves
into teams and man-hauled sledges ashore.

Work on the erection of the hut proceeded
swiftly and well. It was a rectangular structure
with a pitched roof, its walls and roof insulated
by double boarding, packed with quilted
seaweed. Along the north side were the stables.
The south and east sides were given additional
insulation by piles of compressed forage bales.
A larder for frozen meat was tunnelled out of a
compacted snow-drift behind the camp. On
17 January, the expedition members took up
their abode in the hut, less than a fortnight
since their arrival in McMurdo Sound. The
'scientific people' got their work spaces
organized, Bowers built on a store room on the
south side, Ponting worked on his dark-room.
Clissold, the cook, made an excellent beginning
and served seal, penguin and skua in a pleasing
guise.

On 19 January 1911, Scott was able to
write, 'The hut is becoming the most
comfortable dwelling place imaginable. We have
made unto ourselves a truly seductive home,
within the walls of which peace, quiet, and
comfort reign supreme . . . The word "hut" is
misleading. Our residence is really a house of
considerable size, in every respect the finest
that has ever been erected in the Polar regions;
50 feet long by 25 feet wide and 9 feet to the
eaves. If you can picture our house nestling
below this small hill on a long stretch of black
sand, with many tons of provision cases ranged
in neat blocks in front of it and the sea lapping

the icefoot below, you will have some idea of
our immediate vicinity. As for our wider
surroundings it would be difficult to describe
their beauty in sufficiently glowing terms. Cape
Evans is one of the many spurs of Erebus and
the one that stands closest under the mountain,

so that always towering above us we have the grand snowy peak with its smoking summit. North and south of us are deep bays, beyond which great glaciers come rippling over the lower slopes to thrust high blue-walled snouts into the sea. The sea is blue before us, dotted with shining bergs or ice floes, whilst far over the Sound, yet so bold and magnificent as to appear near, stand the beautiful Western Mountains with their numerous lofty peaks, their deep glacial valleys and clear cut scarps, a vision of mountain scenery that can have few rivals.'

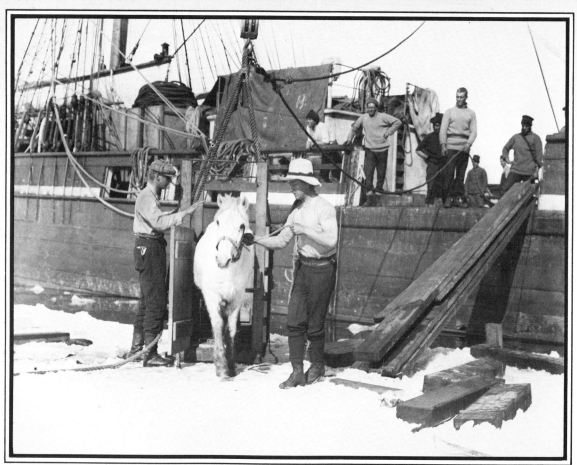

Above: Captain Oates and Seaman Abbott picketing the ponies on the sea ice

Left: Landing one of the ponies at Cape Evans in January

Getting the ill-fated motor sledge off the ship,
8 January

Getting the ill-fated motor sledge off the ship,
8 January

Ponting revelled in all this beauty and would spend all day and most of the night filming and taking pictures in the vicinity of Cape Evans. His delight nearly ended in tragedy. Soon after his arrival in the Antarctic he had an encounter with Killer whales *(Orca gladiator)*, described here in his own words: 'I had noted some fine icebergs frozen into the sea ice about a mile distant. The morning after our arrival, I was just about to start across the ice to visit these bergs, with a sledge well loaded with photographic apparatus, when eight Killer whales appeared, heading towards the ice, blowing loudly. Since first seeing some of these wolves of the sea off Cape Crozier I had been anxious to secure photographs of them. Captain Scott, who also saw the approaching school, called out to me to try and obtain a picture of them, just as I was snatching up my reflex camera for that purpose. The whales dived under the ice, so, hastily estimating where they would be likely to rise again, I ran to the spot—adjusting the camera as I did so. I had got to within six feet of the edge of the ice—which was about a yard thick—when to my consternation it suddenly heaved up under my feet and split into fragments around me; whilst the eight whales, lined up side by side and almost touching each other, burst up from under the ice and blew off steam.

'The head of one was within two yards of me. I saw its nostrils open, and at such close quarters the release of its pent-up breath was like a blast from an air-compressor. The noise of the eight simultaneous blows sounded terrific, and I was enveloped in the warm vapour of the nearest "spout", which had a strong fishy smell. Fortunately the shock sent me backwards, instead of precipitating me into the sea, or my Antarctic experiences would have ended somewhat prematurely.

'As the whales rose from under the ice, there was a loud "booming sound"—to use the expression of Captain Scott, who was a witness of the incident—as they struck the ice with their backs. Immediately they had cleared it, with a rapid movement of their flukes (huge tail fins) they made a tremendous commotion, setting the floe on which I was now isolated rocking so

61

furiously that it was all I could do to keep from falling into the water. Then they turned about with the deliberate intention of attacking me. The ship was within sixty yards, and I heard wild shouts of "Look out!" "Run!" "Jump, man, jump!" "Run, quick!" But I could not run; it was all I could do to keep my feet as I leapt from piece to piece of the rocking ice, with the whales a few yards behind me, snorting and blowing among the ice-blocks. I wondered whether I should be able to reach safety before the whales reached me; and I recollect distinctly thinking, if they did get me, how very unpleasant the first bite would feel, but that it would not matter much about the second.

'The broken floes had already started to drift away with the current, and as I reached the last fragment I saw that I could not jump to the firm ice, for the lead was too wide. The whales behind me were making a horrible noise amongst the broken ice, and I stood for a moment hesitating what to do. More frantic shouts of "Jump, man, jump!" reached me from my friends. Just then, by great good luck, the floe on which I stood turned slightly in the current and lessened the distance. I was able to leap across, not, however, a moment too soon. As I reached security and looked back, a huge black and tawny head was pushed out of the water at the spot, and rested on the ice, looking round with its little pig-like eyes to see what had become of me. The brute opened his jaws wide, and I saw the terrible teeth which I had so narrowly escaped.

'I wasted no time in sprinting the 60 or 70 yards to my sledge, by which Captain Scott was standing. I shall never forget his expression as I reached it in safety. During the next year I saw that same look on his face several times, when someone was in danger. It showed how deeply he felt the responsibility for life, which he thought rested so largely on himself. He was deathly pale as he said to me: "My God! that was about the nearest squeak I ever saw!" '

Scott, who had witnessed the whole incident, described it in his journal. He ended his account with these words: 'One after the other their huge hideous heads shot vertically into the air through the cracks that they had made. As they reared them to a height of 6 or 8 feet it was possible to see their tawny head markings, their small glistening eyes and their terrible array of teeth—by far the largest and most terrifying in the world. There cannot be a doubt that they looked up to see what had happened to Ponting and the dogs. The latter were horribly frightened, and strained at their chains, whining; the head of one Killer must certainly have been within 5 feet of one of the dogs. After this, whether they thought the game insignificant, or whether they missed Ponting is uncertain; but the terrifying creatures passed on to other hunting grounds and we were able to rescue the dogs.

'Of course we have known well that Killer whales continually skirt the edge of the floes, and that they would undoubtedly snap up anyone who was unfortunate enough to fall into the water; but the fact that they could display such deliberate cunning, that they were able to break ice of such thickness (at least $2\frac{1}{2}$ feet), and that they could act in unison, was a revelation to us. It is clear that they are endowed with singular intelligence, and in future we shall treat that intelligence with every respect.'

Preparations for life ashore took less than two weeks and once the stores had been landed and the hut erected, Scott's next preoccupation was to lay a large depot to the south in preparation for the Pole journey the following summer. He had hoped to deposit one ton of provisions and equipment on the 80° parallel of latitude, but owing to bad weather and the tender condition of the ponies, the party only reached latitude 79° 29′ S. Had they been able to achieve their aim, the later tragedy of the Pole party might have been averted. On the way back, Scott received a letter at Hut Point, in the old *Discovery* hut, announcing that the Norwegian explorer Roald Amundsen was established with a great many dogs in the Bay of Whales, an indentation in the Great Ice Barrier. 'There is no doubt that Amundsen's plan is a very serious menace to ours', wrote Scott on 22 February 1911. 'He has a shorter distance to the Pole by 60 miles—I never thought he could have got so many dogs safely to the ice. His plan for running them seems excellent. But above and

Ponting with his cinematograph, 30 January 1912. Scott described him as '. . . sustained by artistic enthusiasm. This world of ours is a different one to him than it is to the rest of us—he gauges it by its picturesqueness—his joy is to reproduce its pictures artistically, his grief to fail to do so'

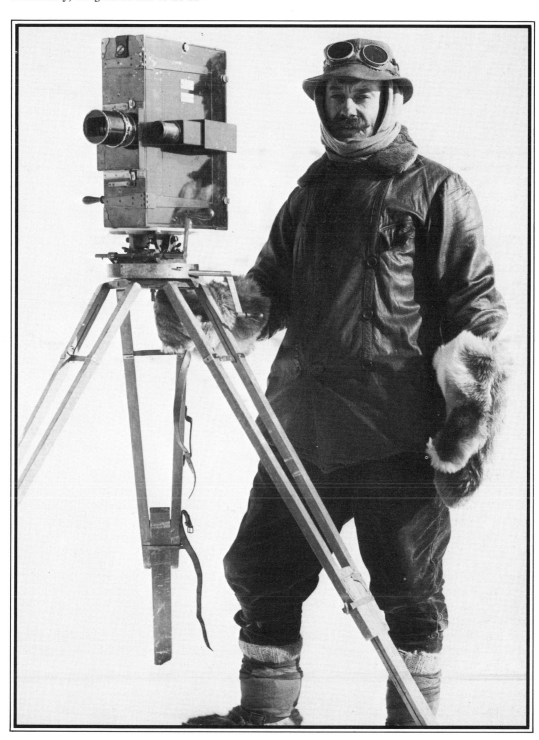

Below: Map of the expedition
Right: Cirrus clouds over the Barne Glacier, Ross
Island, 19 December 1911

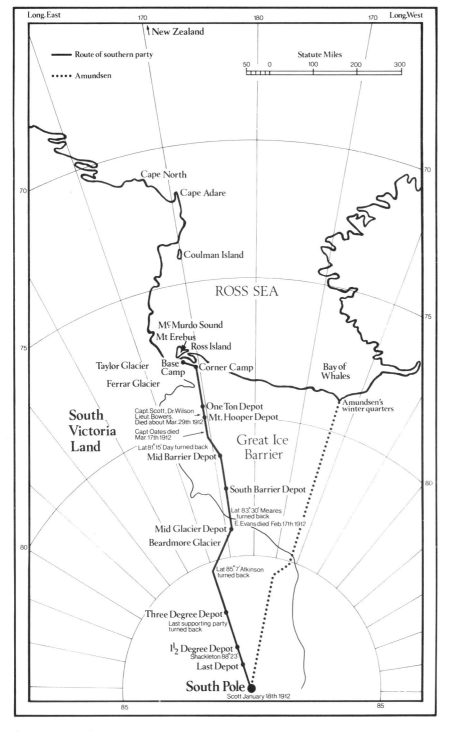

Long. East   170   180   170   Long. West

New Zealand

—— Route of southern party

••••• Amundsen

Statute Miles

50   0   100   200   300

Cape North

Cape Adare

70

Coulman Island

ROSS SEA

75

Mc Murdo Sound

Mt Erebus

Ross Island

Taylor Glacier

Base Camp

Corner Camp

Bay of Whales

Ferrar Glacier

Amundsen's winter quarters

South Victoria Land

One Ton Depot

Capt. Scott, Dr. Wilson Lieut. Bowers. Died about Mar. 29th 1912

Mt. Hooper Depot

Capt Oates died Mar. 17th 1912

Lat 81°15' Day turned back

Mid Barrier Depot

Great Ice Barrier

South Barrier Depot

80

Lat 83° 30' Meares turned back

E. Evans died Feb. 17th 1912

Mid Glacier Depot

Beardmore Glacier

80

Lat 85° 7' Atkinson turned back

Three Degree Depot

Last supporting party turned back

1½ Degree Depot

Shackleton 88°23'

Last Depot

South Pole

Scott January 18th 1912

85   85

beyond all he can start his journey early in the season—an impossible condition with ponies.' Three of Scott's ponies died of exposure on the homeward journey from One Ton Depot. Two more were lost when the sea ice on which they were camped broke up and they were unable to reach firm ice again.

Because the sea ice had gone out and there was no way to Cape Evans, the southern depot laying party and the geologists' party spent some time in the old *Discovery* hut, making it quite habitable again. Scott was impatient, in spite of all their activities. 'But I shall be impatient also in the main hut. It is ill to sit still and contemplate the ruin which has assailed our transport. The scheme of advance must be very different from that which I first contemplated' (17 March 1911). He was also 'losing all faith in the dogs.' The sea obstinately refused to freeze over to make a firm safe road, so the party remained in the *Discovery* hut, Scott being very anxious to get back to see how the hut at Cape Evans had fared during the northerly gales. However, he found time to sketch an agreeable picture of life at Hut Point:

'We gather around the fire seated on packing cases, with a hunk of bread and butter and a steaming pannikin of tea, and life is well worth living. After lunch we are out and about again; there is little to tempt a long stay indoors, and exercise keeps us all the fitter.

'The failing light and approach of supper drives us home again with good appetites about 5 or 6 o'clock, and then the cooks rival one another in preparing succulent dishes of fried seal liver. A single dish may not seem to offer much opportunity of variation, but a lot can be done with a little flour, a handful of raisins, a spoonful of curry powder, or the addition of a little boiled pea meal. Be this as it may, we never tire of our dish and exclamations of satisfaction can be heard every night—or nearly every night . . . After supper we have an hour or so of smoking and conversation—a cheering pleasant hour—in which reminiscences are exchanged by a company which has very literally had world-wide experience . . . An hour or so after supper we tail off one by one, spread out our sleeping-bags, take off our shoes and

creep into comfort, for our reindeer bags are really warm and comfortable now that they have had a chance of drying, and the hut retains some of the heat generated in it. Thanks to the success of the blubber lamps and to a fair supply of candles, we can muster ample light to read for another hour or two, and so tucked up in our furs we study the social and political questions of the past decade. We muster no less than sixteen . . . Everyone can manage eight or nine hours' sleep without a break, and not a few would have little difficulty in sleeping the clock round, which goes to show that our extremely simple life is an exceedingly healthy one, though with faces and hands blackened with smoke, appearances might not lead an outsider to suppose it.'

Scott and eight members of the party managed to reach Cape Evans from Hut Point by 13 April 1911, the Thursday before Easter. Wilson was left behind with Oates and five companions at the *Discovery* hut, waiting for the sea ice to become firm enough to hold the ponies.

The new hut had not been harmed by the northerly winds and swell. 'It was not until I found all safe at the Home Station', wrote Scott on his return, 'that I realised how anxious I had been concerning it. In a normal season no thought of its having been in danger would have occurred to me, but since the loss of the ponies and the breaking of the Glacier Tongue I could not rid myself of the fear that misfortune was in the air and that some abnormal swell had swept the beach; gloomy thoughts of the havoc that might have been wrought by such an event would arise in spite of the sound reasons which had originally led me to choose the site of the hut as a safe one.' The most important events in the quiet life of the station while the southern party were absent were the deaths of one intractable pony 'Hackenschmidt' and the death of one dog; otherwise the hut arrangements had worked well and the routine of scientific observations was in full swing.

On Sunday, 23 April, the sun shone for the last time. A night watchman was instituted, mainly for the purpose of observing the aurora during the long winter night. A series of

Left: Looking to Cape Barne from Cape Evans,
3 March 1911
Below: Telephoto of the 'Church Berg' and the
Western Mountains across McMurdo Sound from
Vane Hill, 27 December 1911

lectures was also started, the first by Wilson on 'Antarctic flying birds', the second by Simpson, the meteorologist, on 'Coronas, halos, rainbows and auroras'. Scott remarks on the way the values of a polar expedition are not those of daily life in the outside world. 'I do not think there can be any life quite so demonstrative of character as that which we had on these expeditions. One sees a remarkable reassortment of values. Under ordinary conditions it is so easy to carry a point with a little bounce; self-assertion is a mask which covers many a weakness. As a rule we have neither the time nor the desire to look beneath it, and so it is that commonly we accept people on their own valuation. Here the outward show is nothing, it is the inward purpose that counts. So the "gods" dwindle and the humble supplant them. Pretence is useless.'

On 13 May, the remaining men, ponies and dogs arrived safely from Hut Point. The wintering party was complete.

Patterns in the ice. 'The rippled snow surface of the icefoot is furrowed in all directions and covered with a briny deposit' (Scott). Below: After a southerly gale, March 1911. Top right: Bergs and floe off Cape Evans, 7 March. Bottom right: The 'Castle Berg' with dog sledge, 17 September 1911

3 Winter Quarters 1911

The expedition members settled down companionably and cheerfully to the months of Antarctic winter in the hut, during which time they would not see the sun. The scientific programme continued, lectures too continued and there was no sign of disharmony at all. Scott was delighted with the amicable spirit in the hut and attributed much of it to the example of patient work and helpfulness set by Edward Wilson.

The regular daily routine became well established and Scott describes it as follows: 'Clissold is up about 7 a.m. to start the breakfast. At 7.30 Hooper starts sweeping the floor and setting the table. Between 8 and 8.30 the men are out and about, fetching ice for melting, etc. Anton is off to feed the ponies, Demetri to see the dogs; Hooper bursts on the slumberers with repeated announcements of the time, usually a quarter of an hour ahead of the clock. There is a stretching of limbs and an interchange of morning greetings, garnished with sleepy humour. Wilson and Bowers meet in a state of nature beside a washing basin filled with snow and proceed to rub glistening limbs with this chilling substance. A little later with less hardihood some others may be seen making the most of a meagre allowance of water. Soon after 8.30 I manage to drag myself from a very comfortable bed and make my toilet with a bare pint of water. By about 10 minutes to 9 my clothes are on, my bed is made, and I sit down to my bowl of porridge; most of the others are gathered about the table by this time, but there are a few laggards who run the 9 o'clock rule very close. The rule is instituted to prevent delay in the day's work, and it has needed a little pressure to keep one or two up to its observance. By 9.20 breakfast is finished, and before the half-hour has struck the table has been cleared. From 9.30 to 1.30 the men are steadily employed on a programme of preparation for sledging, which seems likely to occupy the greater part of the winter. The repair of sleeping-bags and the alteration of tents have already been done, but there are many other tasks uncompleted or not yet begun, such as the manufacture of provision bags, crampons, sealskin soles, pony clothes, etc.

'Hooper has another good sweep up the hut after breakfast, washes the mess traps, and generally tidies things. I think it a good thing that in these matters the officers need not wait on themselves; it gives long unbroken days of scientific work and must, therefore, be an economy of brain in the long run.

'We meet for our mid-day meal at 1.30 or 1.45, and spend a very cheerful half-hour over it. Afterwards the ponies are exercised, weather permitting; this employs all the men and a few of the officers for an hour or more—the rest of us generally take exercise in some form at the same time. After this the officers go on steadily with their work, whilst the men do odd jobs to while away the time. The evening meal, our dinner, comes at 6.30, and is finished within the hour. Afterwards people read, write, or play games, or occasionally finish some piece of work. The gramophone is usually started by some kindly disposed person, and on three nights of the week the lectures to which I have referred are given. These lectures still command full audiences and lively discussions.

'At 11 p.m. the acetylene lights are put out, and those who wish to remain up or to read in bed must depend on candle-light. The majority of candles are extinguished by midnight, and the night watchman alone remains awake to keep his vigil by the light of an oil lamp.

'Day after day passes in this fashion. It is not a very active life perhaps, but certainly not an idle one. Few of us sleep more than eight hours out of the twenty-four.

'On Saturday afternoon or Sunday morning some extra bathing takes place; chins are shaven, and perhaps clean garments donned. Such signs, with the regular Service on Sunday, mark the passage of the weeks.'

One of the highlights of the series of thrice-weekly lectures during the winter months at Cape Evans, was an illustrated talk given by Ponting on Japan, which he had visited probably between 1902 and 1905 during a decade of globe-trotting before joining the Antarctic expedition. The departure of the *Terra Nova* had been memorable to him, not only because it marked the beginning of the expedition, but because his first book *In*

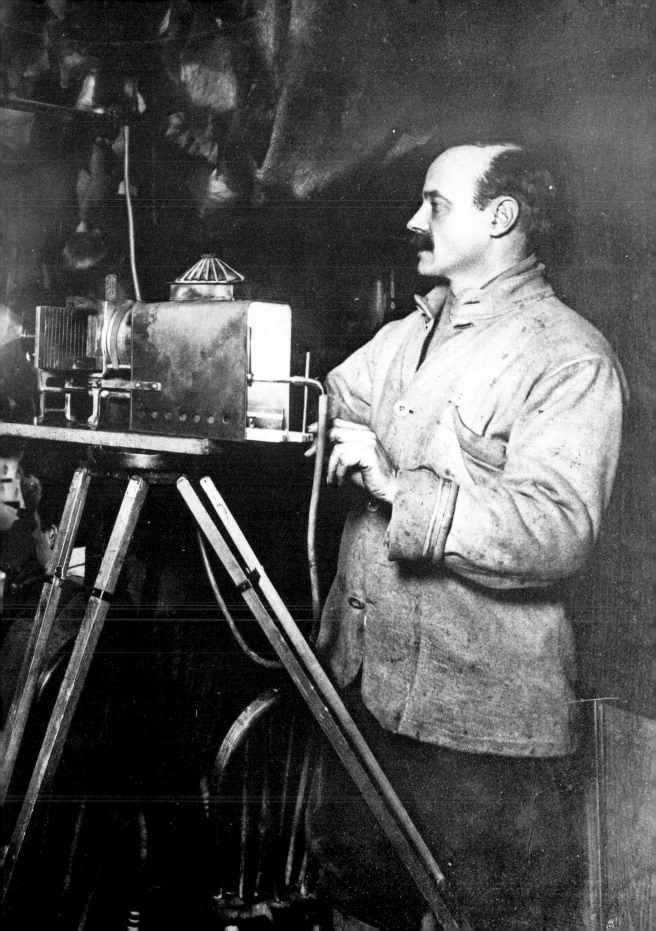

Lotus-land Japan was published that day. During his years there, he became a fervent admirer of the Japanese people and even more of their country.

On 29 May 1911, Scott wrote in his diary,

'Tonight Ponting gave us a charming lecture on Japan with wonderful illustrations of his own. He is happiest in his descriptions of the artistic side of the people, with which he is in fullest sympathy. So he took us to see the flower pageants. The joyful festivals of the cherry blossom, the wistaria, the iris and chrysanthemum, the sombre colours of the beech blossom and the paths about the lotus gardens, where mankind meditated in solemn mood. We had pictures, too, of Nikko and its beauties, of Temples and great Buddhas. Then in more touristy strain of volcanoes and their craters, waterfalls and river gorges, tiny tree-clad islets, that feature of Japan—baths and their bathers, Ainos, and so on. His descriptions were well given and we all of us thoroughly enjoyed our evening.'

Besides all the items that Scott mentions, Ponting especially admired the Japanese temple gardens and describes them well. 'Almost every Japanese temple of any note, that is not framed by Nature's graces, has a garden which their innate love of the beautiful and surpassing skill enables the priests to make a veritable paradise of beauty. They are past masters not only in the art of keeping up a garden, but of allowing it to age with dignity, and yet increase in loveliness without replacing one single feature.' While looking at these illustrations, one may imagine Scott and company enjoying an hour's escape from the long winter to see the beauties of Japan.

Scott's birthday was celebrated on 6 June. 'After my walk I discovered that great preparations were in progress for a special dinner, and when the hour for that meal arrived we sat down to a sumptuous spread with our sledge banners hung about us. Clissold's especially excellent seal soup, roast mutton and red currant jelly, fruit salad, asparagus and chocolate—such was our menu. For drink we had cider cup, a mystery not yet fathomed, some

sherry and a liqueur. After this luxurious meal everyone was very festive and amiably argumentative . . . They are boys, all of them, but such excellent good-natured ones; there has been no sign of sharpness or anger, no jarring note, in all these wordy contests; all end with a laugh. Nelson has offered Taylor a pair of socks to teach him some geology! This lulls me to sleep!'

Midwinter Day was also celebrated in style on 22 June. Scott spoke about the work and future plans. Ponting gave a display of lantern slides made from his own negatives during the expedition. Scott and the rest of the audience were delighted with the show and all cheered vociferously. A set for the Lancers was formed and milk punch drunk. Then Bowers appeared with a home-made Christmas tree on which were presents for all, prepared by a friend of the expedition. 'Thus, except for a few bad heads in the morning, ended the High Festival of Midwinter.' Earlier in the day the first issue of the revived *South Polar Times* (started during the *Discovery* expedition of 1901–4) was presented to Scott by its editor, Cherry-Garrard.

On 27 June, Wilson, Bowers and Cherry-Garrard departed on their mid-winter journey to Cape Crozier to visit the Emperor penguin rookery there at the time when the birds lay their eggs, a phenomenon that had never been observed before. The story of this extraordinary five weeks' sledging may be read in Cherry-Garrard's book *Worst Journey in the World* and in other expedition narratives. Preparations meanwhile continued in the hut for the South Pole journey—new ski boots were designed and Meares made more dog harnesses, while 'Teddy' Evans made maps, the physicists continued their work, Oates rid the ponies of parasites and Ponting printed from his negatives. There were several fierce gales and blizzards. The Cape Crozier party returned on 2 August after enduring for five weeks the hardest conditions on record. They brought back three of the priceless eggs. 'Wilson is disappointed at seeing so little of the penguins', wrote Scott on 2 August, 'but to me and to everyone who has remained here the result of

Expedition members. Below: Captain Scott in his den, 7 October 1911. On the bed is his beloved uniform overcoat, 'spared neither rain, wind, nor salt sea spray, tropic heat nor Arctic cold'

Right: Cherry-Garrard, editor of the *South Polar Times*, 8 June 1911. Scott commented, 'another of the open-air, self-effacing quiet workers; his whole heart is in the life, with profound eagerness to help everyone'

Far right: Dr Wilson working up a sketch, 18 May 1911. He would make pencil sketches out of doors as a basis for water-colours executed in the hut. 'One sees Wilson busy with pencil and colour box, rapidly and steadily adding to his portfolio of charming sketches . . . withal ready and willing to give advice and assistance to others at all times' (Scott)

this effort is the appeal it makes to our imagination as one of the most gallant stories in Polar History. That men should wander forth in the depth of a Polar night to face the most dismal cold and the fiercest gales in darkness is something new; that they should have persisted in this effort in spite of every adversity for five full weeks is heroic. It makes a tale for our generation which I hope may not be lost in the telling.' The party's experience of sledging rations and equipment proved useful in settling some of the points which had arisen in connection with preparation for the main journey to the South Pole.

With the return of the sun towards the end of August, people were able to get out and about more. Afternoon walks became a great pleasure and more outdoor scientific work became possible. On 26 August, Scott wrote, 'Just before lunch the sunshine could be seen gilding the floe, and Ponting and I walked out to the bergs. The nearest one has been overturned and is easily climbed. From the top we could see the sun clear over the rugged outline of C. Barne. It was glorious to stand bathed in brilliant sunshine once more. We felt very young, sang and cheered—we were reminded of a bright frosty morning in England—everything sparkled and the air had the same crisp feel. There is little new to be said of the return of the sun in Polar regions, yet it is such a very real and important event that one cannot pass it in silence. It changes the outlook on life of every individual, foul weather is robbed of its terrors; if it is stormy today it will be fine tomorrow or the next day, and each day's delay will mean a brighter outlook when the sky is clear.'

Below: Debenham (left) and Taylor, the geologists, in their cubicle, 19 May 1911. Of Taylor, Scott wrote, 'Taylor's intellect is omnivorous and versatile—his mind is increasingly active, his grasp wide. Whatever he writes will be of interest—his pen flows well'

Right: Debenham grinding geological specimens, 12 July 1911. 'Here we have a well-trained sturdy worker, with a quiet meaning that carries conviction; he realizes the conceptions of thoroughness and conscientiousness' (Scott)

Previous pages: Nelson, Day and Lashly reading old
magazines round the stove in Shackleton's hut,
17 February 1911. This hut was at Cape Royds and
had been the base of the *Nimrod* expedition, 1907-9

Left: Meares and Oates at the blubber stove,
26 May 1911

Above: Meares, who was in charge of the dogs,
making a dog harness, 19 July 1911. He had travelled
widely before joining the expedition and had been
responsible for obtaining its dogs and ponies. 'The
spirit of the wanderer is in Meares's blood: he has no
happiness but in the wild places of the earth. I have
never met so extreme a type. Even now he is
looking forward to getting away by himself to
Hut Point, tired already of our scant measure of
civilization' (Scott)

Above: Atkinson and Clissold taking in the fish
trap in a temperature of 40° below zero, 28 May 1911
Right: Dr Atkinson, surgeon and parasitologist, in
his laboratory, 15 September 1911. 'Atkinson is
quietly pursuing the subject of parasites. Already
he is in a new world . . . Constantly he comes to ask
me if I would like to see some new form' (Scott)

Below: Simpson, the meteorologist ('Sunny Jim'), taking observations on Vane Hill, March 1911. Scott commented, 'Simpson, master of his craft, untiringly attentive to the working of his numerous self-recording instruments, doing the work of two observers at least'

Right: Debenham with a plane table, for surveying and mapping, 9 September 1911

Left: Wright, the physicist (whose report on glaciology became a classic), November 1911. Of him, Scott wrote, 'Wright, good-hearted, strong, keen, striving to saturate his mind with the ice problems of this wonderful region'

Bottom left: 'Teddy' Evans, surveyor, observing an occulation of Jupiter, June 1911. Scott wrote, 'Evans, with a clear-minded zeal in his own work, does it with all the success of result which comes from the taking of pains'

Below: Nelson, the shore-based biologist, in the 'igloo' (a snow shelter round the ice hole) taking water samples with which he obtained a run of serial temperatures, December 1911. He also made net hauls under the ice

Below: Clissold, 'our excellent cook' making pies. He displayed great ingenuity, not only in his cooking, but in inventing a device to warn him of the rising of the bread, in curing the ailments of Simpson's motor, in making a dog-sledge out of packing cases, and in training the two Eskimo dogs pronounced worthless by Meares

Right: Heinz beans. Many commercial firms helped the expedition by gifts of supplies

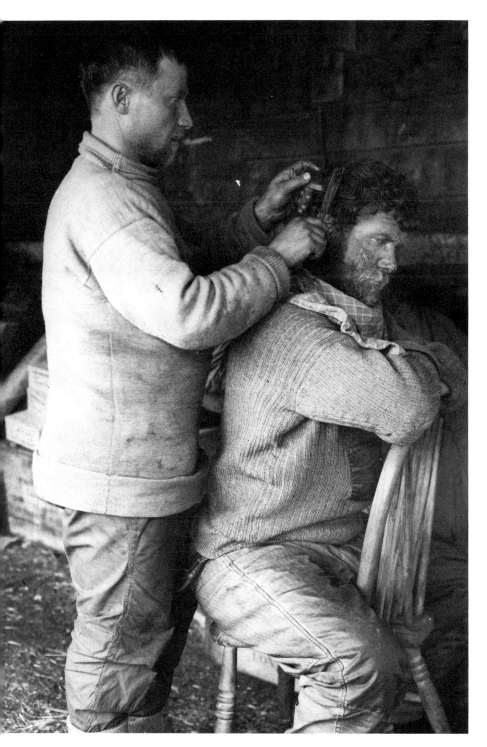

Captain Oates and the ponies in their stable adjoining the main hut, 25 May 1911. Scott wrote, 'Oates's whole heart is in the ponies. He is really devoted to their care and I believe will produce them in the best possible form for the sledging season. Opening out the stores, installing a blubber stove, etc., has kept *him* busy, while his satellite Anton is ever at work in the stables—an excellent little man'

The shore party after the winter. Left to right, standing: Taylor, Cherry-Gerrard, Day, Nelson, Lieutenant 'Teddy' Evans, Oates, Atkinson, Scott, Wright, Keohane, Gran, Lashly, Hooper, Forde, Anton (in front), Demetri; left to right, sitting: Bowers, Meares, Debenham, Wilson, Simpson, Petty Officer Evans, Crean. Ponting (taking the photograph) and Clissold (injured) are absent

the Expedition

Whereas Amundsen took one hundred
Greenland dogs to the Antarctic with him,
Scott took nineteen Manchurian ponies,
thirty-three sledge dogs from Eastern Siberia
and three tracked vehicles. Amundsen discusses
the matter of dogs versus ponies in the early
pages of *The South Pole*, listing the advantages
of the dogs. One of those he mentions is 'that
dog can be fed on dog. One can reduce one's
pack little by little, slaughtering the feebler ones
and feeding the chosen with them. In this way
they get fresh meat.' Scott's grim experiences
during the Southern Journey of the *Discovery*
expedition led him to the opposite view. He
devoted several pages of his narrative to an
impartial consideration of the matter and
concluded with these words: 'This method of
using dogs is one which can only be adopted
with reluctance. One cannot calmly contemplate
the murder of animals which possess such

intelligence and individuality, which have
frequently such endearing qualities, and which
very possibly one has learnt to regard as friends
and companions . . .

'Probably our experience was an exceptionally
sad one in this respect, but it left in each one of
our small party an unconquerable aversion of
the employment of dogs in this ruthless fashion.
We knew well that they had served their end,
that they had carried us much farther than we
could have got by our own exertions; but we all
felt that we would never willingly face a
repetition of such incidents, and when in the
following year I stepped forth in my own
harness, one of a party which was dependent on
human labour alone, it would not be easy
adequately to convey the sense of relief which I
felt in the knowledge that there could be no
recurrence of the horrors of the previous
season.'

There can be no better introduction to Ponting's pictures of the sledge dogs of the expedition than the delightful article by Frank Debenham entitled 'Stareek: the story of a sledge dog', published in the journal *Polar Record* (Cambridge), Vol. 4, No. 25, 1943. It is reproduced here almost in full with the kind permission of his daughter, Miss Barbara Debenham, and of the Editor of the *Polar Record*. The animals were the gift of various schools in the British Isles. Their names and those of the schools are listed in the appendix to volume one of *Scott's Last Expedition*.

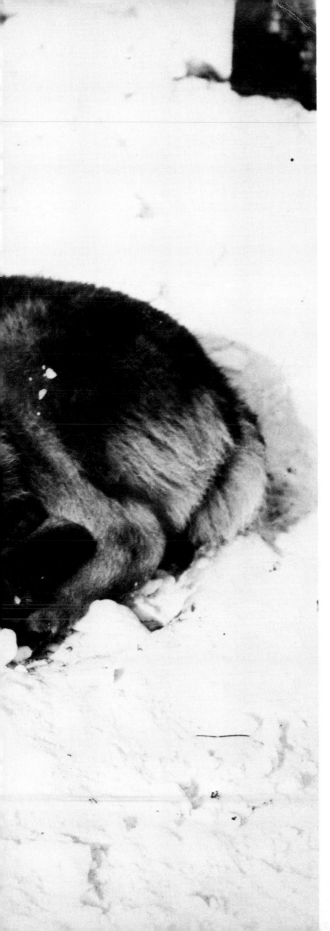

Stareek: the story of a sledge dog, by Frank Debenham

Every expedition which has employed dog transport
will testify to the valiant work performed by their
teams and will be ready with stories about their
more notable dogs. They will tell of dog heroes who
pulled a taut trace to their last breath, of dogs who
lost heart early in the journey, of shy dogs and bold
dogs, of those who were popular with the whole
team and others against whom every fang was
turned. Dog personality is, in fact, one of the first
things a driver learns and the better he learns it the
better driver he will be.

Amongst the dogs of any expedition there will
always be one or two who in character and
performance have towered above their fellows, and
with whom their drivers would willingly share their
honours . . .

Of the forty-five dogs* taken by Captain Scott on
his last expedition (1910–13) all but two were from
Eastern Siberia, where they had been post dogs,
carrying the mail in winter where no other transport
could pass. Though varied in colour and in size as
is the way with sledge dogs, they were on the whole
of a stockier build than the Canadian or West
Greenland breed, whose longer legs might well carry
them faster but hardly farther than their cousins of
Eastern Asia. They were not much given to howling
in concert nor to great enmity amongst themselves,
so that compared to some other expeditions we had
fairly quiet nights, and mass-murders, when a very
unpopular dog was killed by the rest for no reason
that we could discover, were very rare occurrences.

The only time that they were really noisy was
when a man came out of the hut with a dog harness
over his arm and the whole of the dog lines would
leap forward as one dog with full-throated demand
to be selected. The few dogs who could be trusted
off the chain would race up and these would try to
wriggle their heads through the dangling loops of
the harness. For the most part a sledge dog has a
happy life and he enjoys most of his sledge hauling
just as much as the house dog loves his daily walk
round the park or the shepherd's dog his
disciplined labour with the flock. Nor does he really
suffer badly from the weather except when he is
forced to travel into a strong wind. He finds a

* More dogs were brought down in the ship for the
second winter.

blizzard monotonous, but snuggling under the snow which soon covers his coat he is warm enough; indeed the only type of weather which thoroughly annoys him is a temperature above freezing point with its accompanying wet, and in the Antarctic he is spared that.

Even on the voyage down the men soon began to learn the names and the characters of the dogs and to choose those they preferred for one characteristic or another. Captain Scott alone did not voice his preference, but we always suspected that his favourite was Osman, a large black dog who was reputed to be king-dog, that is to say, acknowledged as the most redoubtable fighter. Tough and enduring he proved to be and on one occasion he held up half the weight of ten dogs dangling in their harnesses down a crevass, the men hanging on to the sledge on one side and Osman on the other, and it was at least five minutes before the strain could be taken off his trace. On this occasion two of the dogs struggled free of their harness and fell on to a block of hard snow 65 feet below the surface, and when Scott reached them an hour later at the end of a rope they had curled up and gone to sleep.

Rather more friendly was Lappa ('flop-eared'), who was the inseparable companion of Osman and backed up his sinewy strength with canine intellect.

Demitri, the Siberian dog-boy, seemed to favour the burly but rather dour Volk, who he always insisted was the 'strongest of all the dogs'.

As each dog had his individual character one had a wide choice, and each in turn had his individual adventures, sometimes fatal. One of the more beautiful, Vaida, was described by Scott as 'especially distinguished for his savage temper and generally uncouth manners' on the first journey. But he improved with friendly treatment and three months later earned the note 'he now allows me to rub him and push him about without the slightest protest. He is a strange beast—I imagine so unused to kindness that it took him time to appreciate it.'

Their characters showed up in all kinds of amusing ways, as is evident from a note in Wilson's diary. 'I have a funny little dog, Mukaka, small but very game and a good worker. He is paired with a fat, lazy and very greedy black dog, Nugis by name, and on every march this sprightly little Mukaka will once or twice notice that Nugis is not pulling and will jump over the trace, bite Nugis like a snap, and be back again in his own place before the fat dog knows what has happened.'

Only a small part of their individual adventures is known. Mukaka ('monkey'), for instance, turned back from a journey for some reason to a deserted

hut where I found him a month later, and Julik ('Scamp') was away for a month in the depth of winter, having probably floated away on an ice floe, but turned up in due course and lived to pull his part on the Pole journey.

Amongst these and many more interesting dog personalities Stareek stood out, not so much for his temperament, which was quiet, but for his air of wisdom and his leadership at the head of a team. He was older than most of his companions and had been a trapper's dog on the great Amur river before he took to the mail sledge. Perhaps this more varied life had helped to give him his appearance of vast experience and calm judgment, but his name means 'Old Man' and more probably he was born with that look of solemn wisdom and was therefore so christened by his owner.

In the South his first driver was Dr Edward Wilson, and some extracts from Wilson's diaries and letters will serve as introduction better than words of mine.

'I have a delightful leader, "Stareek" by name— Russian for "Old Man", and he is the most wise old man.' . . . 'He is quite the nicest, quietest, cleverest old dog I have ever come across. He looks in fact as though he knew all the wickedness of all the world and all its cares, and as if he were bored to death by them.' . . . 'Even now, six months after I have had anything to do with him, he never fails to come and speak to me whenever he sees me.'

It was not everyone who took to Stareek and there were those who said that his slightly tip-tilted nose betokened disdain or misanthropy, that his slow walk with a slight limp when he first uncurled himself from rest was malingering, and so on. He was not one to curry favour by extravagant tail-waggings or to go berserk with blood-lust at sight of penguins. He rather kept himself to himself and made no advances to man or dog. If you wanted to make friends with him you had to go more than half-way yourself. After his great adventure it fell to me to have him as my leader, but even without that feat behind him I should have done my best to get behind his barrier of restraint, and in the end I did.

In the first season of depot-laying journeys Stareek was the most reliable of the leaders and, as we have seen, won great praise and affection from Dr Wilson. He was able to meet unexpected mishaps with greater resource and rarely seemed surprised at any new phenomenon. Even the apparently alarming noise of the escaping air when an area of packed snow sank suddenly under the weight of the sledge did not produce panic in him as it did in most of the dogs. Wilson described his reaction in this way.

'There were innumerable subsidences of the surface—the breaking of crusts over air spaces with a hushing sort of noise or muffled report. My leader Stareek thought there was a rabbit under the crust every time one gave way close by him and he would jump sideways with both feet on the spot and his nose in the snow. The action was like a flash and never checked the team.' The 'Barrier Hush', as it came to be called, later became a source of interest to all the dogs and was welcomed by the drivers for that reason.

The general opinion of Stareek at this time is voiced by Scott in a note written towards the end of the depot journey, when different leaders had been tried in the other team. 'Osman is restored to leadership today: it is curious how these leaders come on and go off, all except old Stareek, who remains as steady as ever.'

With such a reputation it was clear that he would be one of the leaders for the two teams who were to accompany the Southern Parties next year. He came through the winter very well, probably because of

his intelligence. But he was getting old, and I remember Meares, who was in command of the dog teams, saying that he wished he could devise a way by which Stareek could lead without using up his strength in pulling. It was his influence on the team as a whole which was so valuable, particularly in the conditions of Barrier travel.

Scott was much interested in the dogs and there are many notes about them in his diary, many of them about the effect of the Barrier on the dogs: 'A dog must be either eating, asleep, or interested. His eagerness to snatch at interest, to chain his attention to something, is almost pathetic! The monotony of marching kills him. This is the fearfullest difficulty for the dog driver on a snow plain without leading marks or objects in sight. The dog is almost human in its demand for living interest, yet fatally less than human in its inability to foresee. A dog lives for the day, the hour, even the moment. The human being can live and support discomfort for a future.' It may well be that Stareek's greater intelligence, or some mental power through which he was not so dependent on external interests, was the secret both of his influence on his team and his resistance to the Barrier *ennui* which attacked the other dogs.

But mental resources could not entirely make up for the failing sinews of age, and when the teams had done some 300 miles of the journey Polewards it was clear that Stareek was near the end of his tether. From this point two men, Day and Hooper, were to return, manhauling their sledge, and Scott decided to send back, under their care, the two dogs which were failing fast, Stareek and Czigane. Though there was no dog food to be spared for them there was a sporting chance that with odd scraps from the men they might get back to the base and live to pull another day. Czigane strongly approved of this turn in his affairs and trotted along beside the men as they turned northwards. Stareek, on the other hand, strongly resented either his deposition or his separation and refused to go. He had to be tied to the sledge and spent most of the first day actively resisting by pulling the wrong way, or escaping and having to be retrieved by chase. By the end of the day two rather exasperated men made up their minds that they would not repeat the performance and Stareek would have to decide for himself. He made the decision during the night by gnawing through his lashing and his tracks showed in the morning that he had gone back to his team. The two men wondered how long it would take him to catch them up and how soon he would have to be killed and fed to his own team: for them that was the end of Stareek.

But he never caught up with the Southern Parties, perhaps because he found they were too far ahead, perhaps because some dog-reasoning told him that after all northward was his best course, and that since loyalty was denied him self-preservation should rank first.

Meanwhile the two men hauled their sledge a regular ten or twelve miles a day with Czigane walking beside them and faring pretty well as far as comfort was concerned; a bed of soft material was made up for him on the sledge each night, and the men went short on biscuit to keep their companion strong enough to get along. They never guessed that somewhere behind on that featureless barren plain a much older dog was doing his best to catch them up, nor could they have done anything had they guessed, since they had to keep up the average pace their ration of provisions prescribed for them.

On the eighteenth night, when they had gone some 200 miles since seeing the last of Stareek, the men camped, now in sight of land though still 100 miles from home. They tucked Czigane up as usual, but their night was much disturbed by Czigane barking instead of sleeping quietly as was his wont, so that the men thought that a wandering skua, 100 miles from the sea, must be flying round.

When in the morning they opened the tent door they saw the cause of Czigane's complaining barks, for he was lying on the less comfortable snow and on the sledge was—Stareek. Or perhaps one should say, the shadow of Stareek, for he was so weak and emaciated that he could not stand up or make more than the feeblest sign of greeting. In almost any other country Stareek, as he reached each camp site, would have been able to sniff round and pick up some small trifle of waste, but not on the Barrier, where not a scrap of nourishment, even of the most nauseating kind, was ever left. Even the excrement of pony, man and dog was cleaned up by the dogs, there was nothing left. It must have been with literally his last ounce of energy—or was it mental grit—that he had staggered into camp in the night and, with the leader's authority still within him, had ordered Czigane off the bed on the sledge. Naturally the men could hardly believe it possible, and they feared that he might have broken into one of the depots of food for the returning parties. This would have been a big task for a weak dog and it was in fact found later that he did not even attempt the task of scraping down piles of snow blocks.

Filled with admiration for such a feat of endurance they pulled him on the sledge for a couple of marches, fed him cautiously and to their great pride he finished the last lap home on his own feet, still very weak but saved.

At first sight one is tempted to sum up this astonishing journey as yet another instance of the endurance of sledge dogs which is always surprising us, and of an instinct which is beyond our comprehension.

Yet that would be a very inadequate explanation, for many other dogs have failed to rejoin their party under similar or easier circumstances. That same summer, only a few hundred miles to the east on the same Barrier, Amundsen lost several dogs who for one reason or other left the teams and never returned. It seems that usually such a 'lost' dog either wanders off the track, presumably in search of food, and fails to find it again, or, reaching one of the camps he has visited before, he stays there till he dies, hoping that the men will come back. Stareek's behaviour therefore at once marks an unusual intelligence, but still more that mental persistence, that refusal to give in which we now express by the word 'guts'. None but a dog of strong character would have continued day after day in his 200-mile pursuit when the simpler way would have been to lie down in the snow and forget his pains in a sleep unto death as many another had done before him.

One wonders whether, as he reached each camp site of the men, his sense of smell gave him some indication that he was catching them up. Beyond that encouragement there could have been nothing but his indomitable will and his unusual brain to spur him on to yet another and another day of forcing his tired body on. It seems probable that at the end he must have been only a little way behind them for several days, because while he was fairly fresh his pace would have been faster than that of men pulling a sledge, whereas later he must have been hard put to it to travel ten miles or so in the day.

Whatever the details of his journey, which must remain mere guesswork, it is clear that only mental strength could have carried him over the last stages; it was a victory of the spirit even more than of muscle.

Back at the base Stareek's recovery was slow but steady, and when I returned some two months later I could at first see very little difference. There was a difference, however, as well there might be, and it took the form of a greater inclination for men's society and less for that of the dogs. He was never unpopular with the other dogs, but he now kept apart from all their mass reactions, and seemed to regard them all as careless adolescents. Nor did he like petting unless it took the form of brushing his coat free from ice; he would move away if you merely patted him for patting's sake. He liked the presence of his men friends but did not want their fussy attentions.

As the light came back with the next spring he would accompany me on my walks, but he would not go far and he would often lie down on a rise, keeping me within sight, and rejoin me as I returned without showing any signs of greeting or affection but merely a certain mild satisfaction in my presence.

Naturally I was very pleased when he was allotted to me as the leader for a team of dogs given to me for short geological journeys near the base. He took no interest whatever in them as a team, probably because it was composed of all the left-overs and misfits from the two 'professional' teams, yet there was no doubt about his authority over them. They followed him implicitly except on those occasions when blood-lust for penguins or seals made them oblivious. His former zest for

sledging had left him and he would no longer wriggle his head into the harness, but on the other hand he would never run away from the harnessing as some dogs did.

We had many minor adventures with this team, through all of which my admiration of Stareek's character grew till I began to regard him as almost human, and longed for the time when I could give him rest and peace in civilisation. Sentiment was not a feeling which could be prominent in any friendship for Stareek, there was too much admiration in it and too little caressing. Nevertheless when I returned from a short absence from the base to find that Stareek had died, only three weeks before the ship was due, it was a real blow. The wise little puppy of the Amur was to remain in that distant land not far from his first and wisest driver, Dr Wilson, and all we could take back was the memory of his great character and a desire to pay tribute to him by telling his story, for he too deserves a place in the roll of honour of the great dogs in sledging history.

THE PONIES

The ponies were assembled at Vladivostok by C. H. Meares and W. M. Bruce. They were all white or dappled grey in colour, owing to the stress laid by Shackleton upon the importance of light colouring from his experience during the *Nimrod* expedition of 1907–9. They stood about fourteen to fifteen hands. They were brought from Vladivostok to New Zealand by cargo steamer with Anton Omelchenko, a Russian groom, in charge of them.

The following account of the journey with the dogs and ponies from Vladivostok to New Zealand is by W. M. Bruce. It first appeared in *Blue Peter*, June 1932.

On 26 July [1910], we shipped our ponies and dogs on the small Japanese steamer *Tategami Maru*. The shipment was a dreadful experience, rain was falling in torrents, the streets and quays many inches deep in mud. The ponies were obstreperous, two of them breaking away twice. We had three Russian grooms, two for the ponies and one for the dogs.

Anton, one of the grooms, recaptured the truant ponies on each occasion. When, for the second time, he had recaptured them, I had got a long rope led through the horse-box in which they were to be hoisted on board, and manned it at the ship end with three or four heavy men. Whilst trying to fasten the other end to a pony's head, with Anton sitting on its back, the pony reared right up on its hind legs, and before I could dodge clear, came down with one foreleg on each of my shoulders. I was much less hurt than I should have expected, as the ponies were not shod.

We had been treating them very gently and carefully till then, and I am afraid had wasted a good deal of time in consequence, but, after this incident, we used brute force.

One pony was left behind, under suspicion of glanders, though they had all been previously through the Mallein test. We had started the shipment about 7 a.m., thinking we should finish in about two hours, and then have breakfast. It was after 4 p.m. when we got our first meal, wet through to the skin, and absolutely covered in mud from head to foot.

The ship left next day, on a very leisurely voyage, calling at four ports in Corea, and arrived at Kobé on 4 August.

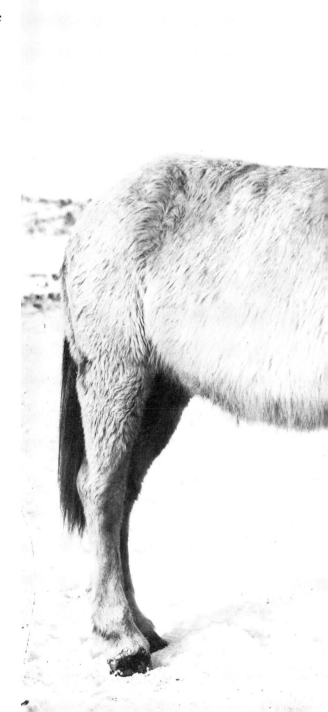

By this time, Meares had emptied his purse, but I was well known here, and had no difficulty in obtaining the necessary money to carry us on.

Here we had to tranship the ponies and dogs to another vessel. No British shipping company would carry us, so we left two days later in the German steamer *Prinz Waldemar*. She was a passenger ship, and we were far from popular on board. I must own, though we did our best to keep everything as clean as possible, the dogs were far from savoury, and quite frequently would howl in unison in the middle of the night, keeping it up for quite a long time. Our unpopularity can, therefore, be understood.

The ship was very slow, the voyage not very interesting, but the weather was fine, which was a great asset, and our fellow passengers cheerful company.

We called at Hong Kong, Manila, a little coral island called Yap, where there was a German wireless station, several ports in New Guinea, Raboul, Rockhampton and Brisbane and reached Sydney on 9 September.

The Governor of Queensland brought a party on board to see the ponies and dogs, and that was only the beginning, for afterwards—in every port—crowds of people came to see them, although they were only very ordinary ponies, and rather exceptionally fierce dogs.

We transhipped all our ponies and dogs again to the New Zealand steamer *Moana*, the Sydney officials—very unnecessarily, we thought—insisting that the former should again all be tested for glanders, although they were not even landed in the port.

We left next day for Wellington, and again were lucky in our weather and arrived there on the 14th. Once more we had to change ships, and joined the *Maori*, for Lyttelton, sailing the same evening.

We had become experts at the business by this time, but the ponies appeared to get more and more frightened on each occasion. We had to blindfold them now before they were hoisted out of or into a ship, and as I was covering up the head of one in Wellington, he struggled so much, and threw his head about so quickly, that I arrived in Lyttelton next day with black eyes and a swollen nose.

The ponies had now been on their legs for fifty-two days, as we never allowed them to lie down. It seemed cruel, but all the experts were agreed that it was the right thing to do. Sometimes, if a pony seemed to be distressed by the slight movement of the ship, we passed a band under him, but it was never very successful.

We were very much surprised at the skittishness they showed when they were landed at the quarantine station on Quail Island in Lyttelton Harbour, for although they were quite uncertain on their legs, they fought and kicked each other on every possible occasion until we got them apart.

Captain L. E. G. Oates of the Inniskilling Dragoons, a cavalry regiment, took over in Lyttelton. Scott planned to rely much more upon the ponies for transport during the dash to the South Pole than upon the dogs or motor sledges. It was of deepest concern to him when their numbers were reduced by deaths from nineteen to ten by June 1911. Those left were James Pigg, Bones, Michael, Snatcher, Jehu, Chinaman, Christopher, Victor, Snippets and Nobby. During the winter they were kept in stables adjoining the hut. Scott paints an amusing picture of their behaviour in his diary for 10 August 1910: 'The ponies are very fit but inclined to be troublesome: the quiet beasts develop tricks without rhyme or reason. Chinaman still kicks and squeals at night. Anton's theory is that he does it to warm himself, and perhaps there is something in it. When eating snow he habitually takes too large a mouthful and swallows it; it is comic to watch him, because when the snow chills his inside he shuffles about with all four legs and wears a most fretful, aggrieved expression: but no sooner has the snow melted than he seizes another mouthful. Other ponies take small mouthfuls or melt a large one on their tongues— this act also produces an amusing expression. Victor and Snippets are confirmed wind-suckers. They are at it all the time when the manger board is in place, but it is taken down immediately after feeding time, and then they can only seek vainly for something to catch hold of with their teeth. "Bones" has taken to kicking at night for no imaginable reason. He hammers away at the back of his stall merrily; we have covered the boards with several layers of sacking, so that the noise is cured, if not the habit. The annoying part of these tricks is that they hold the possibility of damage to the pony.'

Scott summarizes Oates's lecture on the ponies in his diary entry for 11 August 1911. 'After a few hints on leading, the lecturer talked of possible improvements in our wintering arrangements. A loose box for each animal would be an advantage, and a small amount of litter on which he could lie down. Some of our ponies lie down, but rarely for more than 10 minutes—the Soldier [Oates]

thinks they find the ground too cold. He thinks it would be wise to clip animals before the winter set in. He is in doubt as to the advisability of grooming. He passed to the improvements preparing for the coming journey —the nose bags, picketing lines, and rugs. He proposes to bandage the legs of all ponies. Finally he dealt with the difficult subjects of snow-blindness and soft surfaces: for the first he suggested dyeing the forelocks, which have now grown quite long.' The discussion which followed hinged mainly on snow-blindness and its prevention. But Scott remarks in his diary that 'the snow-shoe problem is much more serious.' There is a report on the ponies (and also on the mules from the Himalayas brought down for the second winter) in the published expedition results (*Miscellaneous data*, 1924). All the ponies were taken on the southern journey, but only across the Barrier, not up the glacier to the plateau.

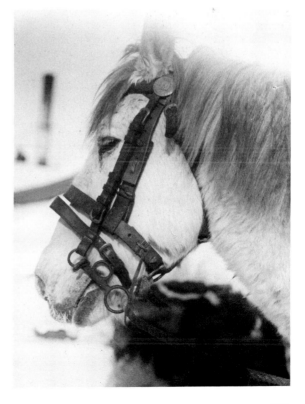

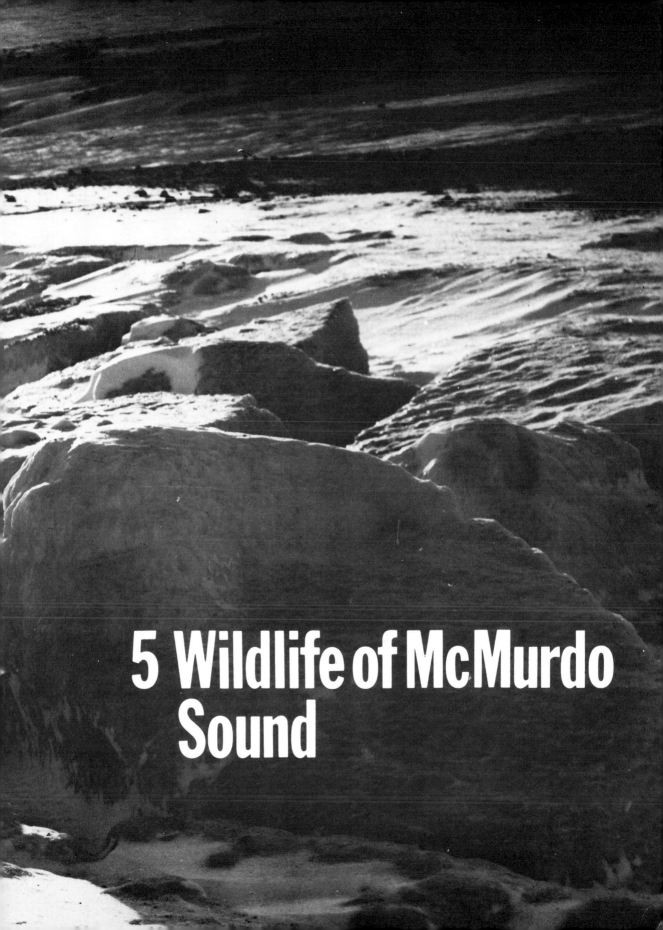

5 Wildlife of McMurdo Sound

With the return of the sun, Ponting was able to
get out and about to photograph the seals,
penguins and other creatures that made their
homes not far from the expedition's base camp.
He had hoped to sledge over to the western side
of McMurdo Sound during the Antarctic
summer, but was unable to do so for various
reasons. He had therefore to content himself
with studies made nearer to winter quarters.
His activities are described in detail in the later
chapters of *The Great White South*. He was
able to photograph the Weddell seal rookery on
Razorback Island, where the baby seals are born
about the end of October. They were then about
a yard long, with thick soft woolly coats
'sometimes cream-coloured all over, but more
usually fawn, graduating to black at the tail
flippers . . . When they were about a week or so
old, they loved to play pranks on their snoozing
mothers; they would nose and romp about
them, and bite them playfully—the mother
sometimes waking up and joining in the game.'
The bull Weddell seals are much larger than the
females. Although generally harmless to man,
they can be roused by the foolhardy and
Ponting tells of two instances when he and his
camera had to put an end to portrait-making and
run. The enemy of the seals is the Killer whale.
Ponting describes how he once saw a school of
them cruising along by the icefoot in search of
seals. 'There were about a dozen and some of
them must have been huge fellows, judging
from the height of their dorsal fins, which
projected 5 or 6 feet above the water. The
sinister shapes rose and sank and rose again, as
the evil creatures moved along—a small forest of
spouts preceding each appearance of the fins.
Suddenly a big cow Weddell shot out of the
water ahead of the whales and landed with a
resounding smack on the ice. Instead of
shuffling off to safety, the terrified animal
immediately turned round and, bellowing
loudly, hung over the ice edge, peering into the
water. I wondered what such madness meant;
but in a moment a baby seal appeared, and
made frantic efforts to struggle out to join its
mother. Frenzied with fear for the life of her
little one, the mother rushed back and forth
distractedly, as she saw the heaving fins drawing

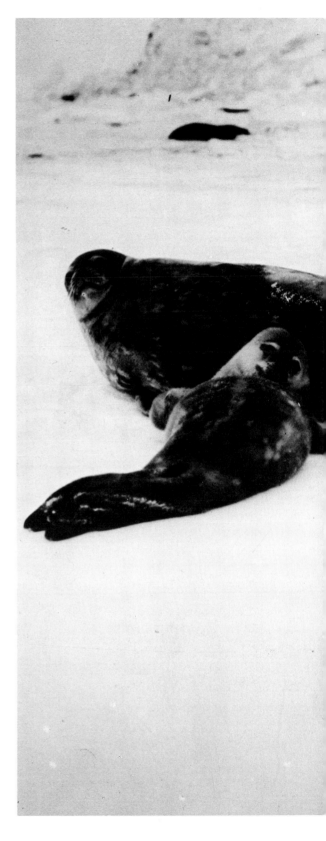

momentarily nearer; whilst the baby, piteously bleating, with its little paddles on the ice edge, struggled in vain to get its body out of water. When the ill-omened rising, sinking fins were within a dozen yards, the mother rushed and leapt into the water, almost on to the very top of them. I thought she had sprung to certain death; but, with one accord the rhythmical fins now moved outward from the ice and then I knew that this was but a ruse on the part of the mother to lure the dreadful creatures from her baby. A minute later the cluster of fins turned again towards the ice and almost simultaneously the mother reappeared and leapt out of the water again twenty yards in front of them— close to the bleating, struggling baby. Bellowing loudly, she pushed her nose right into the little one's face, as though in a last despairing caress; then she seemed to try to pull it out of danger with her teeth. Again the devilish fins

approached and once again the mother sprang into the very jaws of death—risking her own life without a moment's hesitation to act as a decoy to save her little one. Again the stratagem succeeded and the fins turned away once more; meanwhile the bleating baby vainly kept on straining to get out. The mother now appeared again, not, however, this time to leap on to the ice, but to try and heave the baby out upon her back. The dorsal fins had turned about again and I held my breath for the tensity of my nerves, as the devoted mother lifted the baby clear out of the water, and had it within an inch of safety, when the poor little chap, clawing madly with its flippers, rolled off her shoulders into the sea, and both mother and baby disappeared—not five yards ahead of the nearest of the *Orcas*, as they rose to sound and then followed their quarry under the ice sheet.' Neither prey nor predators reappeared.

Weddell seals. Below: Mother and her young, taken at Razorback Island, 9 November 1911 and (bottom) an adult at Cape Evans. Right: In a breathing hole in the sea ice

The expedition's acquaintance with the
Adélie penguin began in the pack on the way
south in the *Terra Nova*. Ponting's main
studies of this comic and lively inhabitant of the
Antarctic took place at Cape Royds, some seven
or eight miles north of Cape Evans whence
occasional 'small roving parties would come
and inspect our Hut, our stores, sledging gear
and the dogs. The dogs were a never-ending
source of wonder and inspired in them no fear
whatever. In their desire to examine more
closely these wild beasts . . . they sometimes
lost their lives by the merciless teeth.'
    The Adélie stands about two feet high and is
characterized by white rims round its eyes and
by white eyelids. Ponting gives an amusing
account of a first meeting with these
'comedians of the South': 'You are out on the
ice, when you meet a company of marionettes,
dressed in swallow-tail coats with an excessive
expanse of shirt-front . . . You become an
object of interest. Each marionette suddenly
stands to attention; and the floppy clothes
immediately become the most beautifully-
tailored and "spic-and-span" of garments.' A
spokesman squawks a challenge. 'The squawk is
not difficult to imitate and, if you are wise, you
attempt to do so. You find your effort has an
appeasing effect, for it proclaims your kinship,
though you are not understood and are probably
regarded as something of a fool. The whole
party then advance to inspect you, squawking
their opinions to each other. It is well to get in a
few bows at this time and to affect the air of an
Emperor, muttering after the manner of their
kind as you do so. You will find that such
efforts are well received, though doubtless
considered loutish.' But if you manage to give
offence in some way, the Adélie 'will seize your
nether garments above the knee in his beak and
lay about you with such a rapid rain of blows
with his flippers . . . that unless you cry mercy
and beat him off, you will find yourself bruised
black and blue.'
    During the third week in November, Ponting
and Nelson, the biologist, left the hut to camp
at Cape Royds and make the first of several
visits to observe the penguins there. They were
amused at the continuous thieving of stones for

Adélie penguins. Below: In ecstasy. Bottom right:
An Adélie about to turn her eggs, November 1911,
and (top right) mother and chicks, 9 January 1912

Above: Pair of Adélie penguins
Right: The icefoot, looking towards Cape Royds,
from the *Terra Nova*, January 1911

the nests which took place and watched many a fight between quarrelling males and females. 'One day I watched a young newly-mated pair who were obviously inexperienced in the ways of the world and trustful of their fellow-creatures to a point of folly. After the stone-offering preliminaries had been gone through and they had abandoned themselves for a time to a state of rapture, they began to set about the building of the nest. The male bird went in search of stones; and as each fresh one was added, the hen sat upon them and adjusted them, in the customary manner, by wriggling and with her feet. When about twenty stones had been accumulated, a knavish-looking fellow —one of a pair of older newly-mateds who were settling in the vicinity—spotted the treasures. Sneaking up behind the young hen, he quietly made off with one of them, without being noticed. Then as fast as the young and honest husband added a fresh stone and departed to continue his search, the thief crept up again and stole another; and sometimes he managed to purloin two or three stones whilst the honest husband was finding one. This went on for an hour or more and as the thief's wife had extraordinary ability in arranging the stones, the nest of the dishonest ones became a little castle, whilst the virtuous pair were gradually deprived of everything they had. After a time, the honest husband took a rest to inspect the fruit of his labours and was obviously troubled to find no visible result. A good deal of discussion ensued between the pair, neither of whom seemed capable of comprehending the trick that had been played upon them . . . If a thief were detected in the act, he would usually brazen it out and dash off with the prize. But sometimes he would drop the stone as though it were red-hot—pretending to be interested in the weather, or else his toe-nails, or anything else on earth except the stone he coveted—with an assumed expression of innocence that was too funny for words.'

The two enemies of the Adélie penguin are the sea leopard, which lies in wait in the sea by the icefoot for the penguins to jump in, and the skua gull, which plunders the penguins' nest of eggs and is ever ready to pounce on

Below: Skua gulls, male and female, the birds which Ponting called the 'buccaneers of the south'. Skua gulls scavenging a seal skin (left)

Bottom: Dead Sea Leopard, 28 May 1911, photographed by flashlight. Its long lithe body contrasts with those of the fat Weddell seals

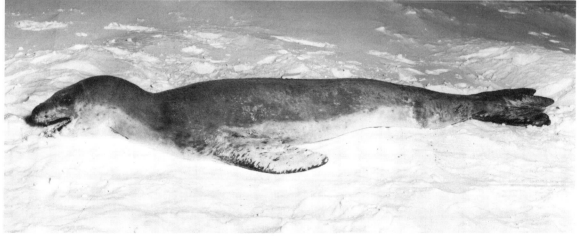

Below: The three Emperor penguin's eggs brought
from Cape Crozier by Wilson, Bowers and Cherry-
Garrard, midwinter, 1911
Right: Emperor penguin

young chicks. Ponting captured on film some
remarkable shots of the gull actually stealing an
egg. When the penguin eggs hatched, the
penguin colony took on 'an aspect of bustling
activity. There were many hundreds of little
stomachs to be kept filled . . . The parent birds
went about the work with a most business-like
air. An intermittent stream of individuals
proceeded sea-wards for food; whilst another
stream, swollen with the loads they bore,
flowed landwards', tramping over the sea ice. At
about four weeks old, the downy chicks start to
moult and gradually become black and white
like their parents. They then make for the sea
and after some hesitation, plunge headlong into
it, eventually making their way northwards for
the winter.

Only Wilson, Cherry-Garrard and Bowers
made the winter journey to Cape Crozier to
visit the Emperor penguins during the breeding
season, when the birds incubate their eggs in a
special crease in the lower abdomen, standing on
the ice. So the rest of the party only saw three

of these birds at Cape Evans before the winter
began. The Emperor penguin is the largest of
all the penguins. It weighs about eighty pounds
and stands about four feet high. Ponting
describes meeting his first Emperor penguin on
the new ice near some grounded icebergs. The
penguin first bowed, gazed at him, advanced
within two yards and uttered a short speech, in
penguin language, accompanied by more
punctilious bowing. His trust was met with
treachery, for Ponting, Anton and Clissold
captured him with difficulty and took him
protesting to the hut, 'where under the
influence of an anaesthetic, he joined our
zoological collection. We softened the qualms of
conscience . . . with the thought that science
demanded the despicable act. Our captive was a
fine specimen . . . in beautiful plumage, with a
snowy white breast and grey-black back and
there was a collar of orange merging into yellow
about his throat. The feet, head and eyes were
raven black and the long curved beak was
edged with violet.'

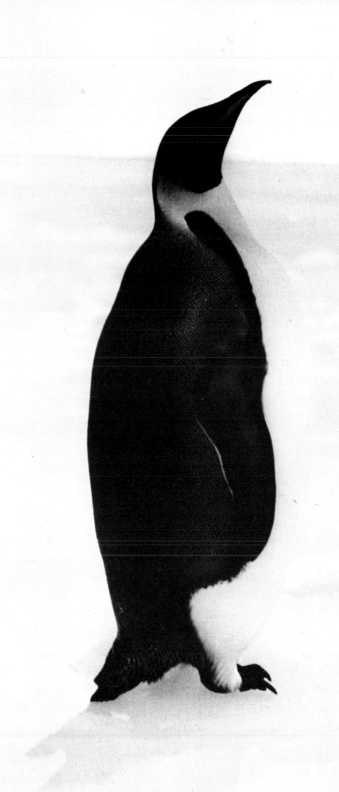

Seals basking on pancake ice floes

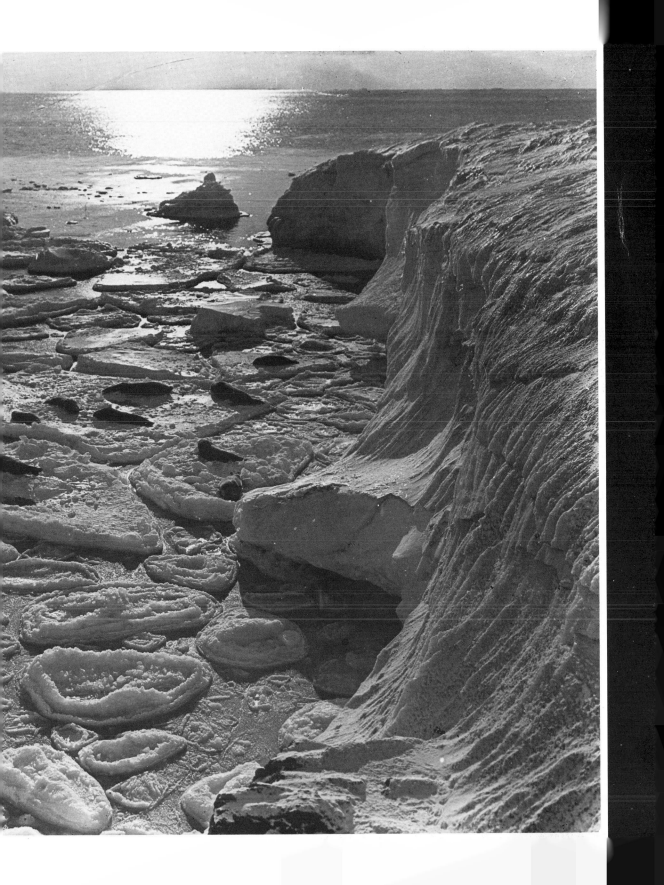

6 The South Pole

Although the *Terra Nova* expedition was planned to make both scientific observations and geographical discoveries, its target in popular estimation was the South Pole—one of the most desolate spots on earth—latitude 90° South on a plateau of ice some ten thousand feet above sea level, at the bottom of the world.

During the *Discovery* expedition of 1901–4, Scott had pioneered the route to the south from Ross Island over the 'Great Ice Barrier' (the floating Ross Ice Shelf) as far as Cape Wilson in latitude 82° 16′ 33″ South. Shackleton next made a tremendous journey to within ninety-seven miles of the South Pole up the great Beardmore Glacier on to the ice sheet during the *Nimrod* expedition of 1907–9. Thus it was left to Scott during the *Terra Nova* expedition not only to cover the remaining ninety-seven

Below: Captain Scott (centre) and the Southern
Party just before leaving on the southern journey,
26 January 1911

miles, but to get to the South Pole *before* the
Norwegian Amundsen, whose surprise
appearance in the Bay of Whales has been
previously mentioned. Amundsen had planned
an expedition in the *Fram* to reach the North
Pole, but had been deterred from a northern
expedition by the announcement in September
1909 that Peary had got there first. He therefore
determined to go south, but kept his plans

secret, believing that there was no need to
inform Scott at an early date, because 'the
British expedition was designed entirely for
scientific research. The Pole was only a
side-issue, whereas in my extended plan it was
the main object.'

On hearing the news, Scott did in fact
determine not to make a race of it and change
all his plans, but he was of course still keen to

Below: The motor party: Lieutenant 'Teddy' Evans,
Day, Lashly and Hooper, by one of the motor
sledges and (top right) Wright and Bowers packing
sledges for the southern journey, November 1911
Bottom right: Day and one of the motors with
Mount Erebus in the background, October 1911

Top: Film still of a manhauling sledge party
Bottom left: Pitching a tent. The snow block is to weigh down the edge of the tent (film still)
Bottom right: Hoosh-up! Mealtime in the tent of the Pole party. Left to right: Evans, Bowers, Wilson and Scott

get there first. The two expeditions differed in their forms of transport: dogs (with expert dog drivers) were Amundsen's; Manchurian ponies, supplemented by dog teams, tracked motor vehicles and finally man-hauling, were Scott's. Both parties relied on depots laid on the southern routes in the autumn of their arrivals in the Antarctic and during the southern journeys. Amundsen was able to establish autumn depots as far as 82° S from 'Framheim', his base on the Bay of Whales. The following summer, he left on 19 October 1911 with four companions, four sledges and fifty-two dogs. They crossed the ice shelf, ascended the unknown Axel Heiberg Glacier, and reached the South Pole on 17 December 1911. Amundsen was back at 'Framheim' on 25 January 1912 with his four companions, but with only two sledges and eleven dogs, 'men and animals all hale and hearty'.

Scott's two motor sledges left on 24 October. They made slow progress with frequent stops. 'I find myself immensely eager that these tractors should succeed', he wrote, 'even though they may not be of great help to our southern advance. A small measure of success will be enough to show their possibilities, their ability to revolutionize Polar transport.' He was right, of course, and tracked vehicles have since been much used in the Antarctic.

Before the main parties left on 1 November, Ponting was able to take some films of camp life, with Scott and others in sledging kit. He was also able to photograph the southern party as far as Safety Camp.

The motor sledges lasted for less than a week. The ten ponies plodded south with their loads and were shot when their useful life was over and cached as dog food. The last ponies were shot at the foot of the Beardmore Glacier in 'Shambles Camp'. The weather proved very disappointing and blizzards and soft snow delayed the march south. The dogs and the various other supporting parties were sent back at intervals, until on 4 January 1912, beyond the Beardmore Glacier, one hundred and fifty miles from the Pole, Scott sent back 'Teddy' Evans, Lashly and Crean and retained Wilson, Oates, Bowers and Edgar Evans for the last stretch.

Members of the southern party. Lieutenant H. R. Bowers. 'During the southern journey, little Bowers remains a marvel . . . Nothing comes amiss to him and no work is too hard' (Scott)

Captain L. E. G. Oates. His feet were dreadfully frostbitten during the southern journey, but, despite this, he struggled on. He went out into the blizzard to die, so as no longer to hinder his companions on the march

Petty Officer Edgar Evans. During the southern journey Scott wrote of him, 'a giant worker with a really remarkable headpiece. It is only now that I realize how much has been due to him.' He died at the foot of the Beardmore Glacier during the return march from the Pole

Dr E. A. Wilson, April 1911. Scott wrote, 'Words must always fail me when I talk of Bill Wilson. I believe he really is the finest character I ever met.' As doctor during the southern journey, he was always on the look-out to alleviate the pains and troubles of the party and he sacrificed himself to attend to Oates's feet

Previous pages: Sastrugi. This sort of irregular
surface makes difficult travelling. The Pole party
met much of it
Camp at the Gateway at the bottom of the
Beardmore Glacier. View from the north
(photographer not known)

They marched on skis* over the frozen waves of sastrugi at a height of nearly ten thousand feet until on Tuesday, 16 January, they found (in Scott's words) 'a black flag tied to a sledge bearer; sledge tracks and ski-tracks going and coming and the clear trace of dogs' paws—many dogs. This told us the whole story. The Norwegians have forestalled us and are first at the Pole. It is a terrible disappointment, and I am very sorry for my loyal companions . . .' They reached the South Pole on 17 January in bitterly cold, damp weather against a head wind force four to five. 'Great God!', wrote Scott, 'this is an awful place and terrible enough for us to have laboured to it without the reward of priority.' They had a 'fat Polar hoosh', despite their chagrin and the next day came across a Norwegian tent. In it were the names of those who had been there and a note from Amundsen to Scott, asking him to forward a letter to King Haakon of Norway. 'We built a cairn, put up our poor slighted Union Jack and photographed ourselves—mighty cold work all of it . . . Well, we have turned our back on the goal of our ambition and must face our 800 miles of solid dragging—and good-bye to most of the day-dreams!'

They were unable to complete those eight hundred miles. Evans died at the foot of the Beardmore Glacier. Oates walked to his death in a blizzard, to save his comrades, eighteen miles south of the last camp of Scott, Wilson and Bowers, who themselves died in their tent of cold and starvation, prevented by the blizzard from struggling the last eleven miles to One Ton Depot, where they would have found food and fuel.

Scott's diary tells the story of those last days on the Barrier:

Sunday, 4 March—Lunch. Things looking *very* black indeed. As usual we forgot our trouble last night, got into our bags, slept splendidly on good hoosh, woke and had another, and started marching. Sun shining brightly, tracks clear, but surface covered with sandy frost-rime. All the morning we had to pull with all our strength, and in $4\frac{1}{2}$ hours we covered $3\frac{1}{2}$ miles. Last night it was overcast and thick, surface bad; this morning sun shining and surface as bad as ever. One has little to hope for except perhaps strong dry wind—an unlikely

contingency at this time of year. Under the immediate surface crystals is a hard sastrugi surface, which must have been excellent for pulling a week or two ago. We are about 42 miles from the next depot and have a week's food, but only about 3 to 4 days' fuel—we are as economical of the latter as one can possibly be, and we cannot afford to save food and pull as we are pulling. We are in a very tight place indeed, but none of us despondent *yet*, or at least we preserve every semblance of good cheer, but one's heart sinks as the sledge stops dead at some sastrugi behind which the surface sand lies thickly heaped. For the moment the temperature is on the $-20°$—an improvement which makes us much more comfortable, but a colder snap is bound to come again soon. I fear that Oates at least will weather such an event very poorly. Providence to our aid! We can expect little from man now except the possibility of extra food at the next depot. It will be real bad if we get there and find the same shortage of oil. Shall we get there? Such a short distance it would have appeared to us on the summit! I don't know what I should do if Wilson and Bowers weren't so determinedly cheerful over things.

Monday, 5 March—Lunch. Regret to say going from bad to worse. We got a slant of wind yesterday afternoon, and going on 5 hours we converted our wretched morning run of $3\frac{1}{2}$ miles into something over 9. We went to bed on a cup of cocoa and pemmican solid with the chill off. The result is telling on all, but mainly on Oates, whose feet are in a wretched condition. One swelled up tremendously last night and he is very lame this morning. We started march on tea and pemmican as last night— we pretend to prefer the pemmican this way. Marched for 5 hours this morning over a slightly better surface covered with high moundy sastrugi. Sledge capsized twice; we pulled on foot, covering about $5\frac{1}{2}$ miles. We are two pony marches and 4 miles about from our depot. Our fuel dreadfully low and the poor Soldier nearly done. It is pathetic enough because we can do nothing for him; more hot food might do a little, but only a little, I fear. We none of us expected these terribly low temperatures, and of the rest of us Wilson is feeling them most; mainly, I fear, from his self-sacrificing devotion in doctoring Oates's feet. We cannot help each other, each has enough to do to take care of himself. We get cold on the march when the trudging is heavy, and the wind pierces our warm garments. The others, all of them, are unendingly cheerful when in the tent. We mean to see the game through with a proper spirit, but it's tough work to

---

* Except for Bowers, who had cached his earlier on the march. Scott's surprise decision to take Bowers was one of the causes of the final tragedy. The tents were four-man tents; rations and fuel were made up for parties of four.

be pulling harder than we ever pulled in our lives for long hours, and to feel that the progress is so slow. One can only say 'God help us!' and plod on our weary way, cold and very miserable, though outwardly cheerful. We talk of all sorts of subjects in the tent, not much of food now, since we decided to take the risk of running a full ration. We simply couldn't go hungry at this time.

Tuesday, 6 March—Lunch. We did a little better with help of wind yesterday afternoon, finishing 9½ miles for the day, and 27 miles from depot. But this morning things have been awful. It was warm in the night and for the first time during the journey I overslept myself by more than an hour; then we were slow with foot gear; then, pulling with all our might (for our lives) we could scarcely advance at rate of a mile an hour; then it grew thick and three times we had to get out of harness to search for tracks. The result is something less than 3½ miles for the forenoon. The sun is shining now and the wind gone. Poor Oates is unable to pull, sits on the sledge when we are track-searching —he is wonderfully plucky, as his feet must be giving him great pain. He makes no complaint, but

his spirits only come up in spurts now, and he grows more silent in the tent. We are making a spirit lamp to try and replace the primus when our oil is exhausted. It will be a very poor substitute and we've not got much spirit. If we could have kept up our 9-mile days we might have got within reasonable distance of the depot before running out, but nothing but a strong wind and good surface can help us now, and though we had quite a good breeze this morning, the sledge came as heavy as lead. If we were all fit I should have hopes of getting through, but the poor Soldier has become a terrible hindrance, though he does his utmost and suffers much I fear.

Wednesday, 7 March—A little worse I fear. One of Oates's feet *very* bad this morning; he is wonderfully brave. We still talk of what we will do together at home.

We only made 6½ miles yesterday. This morning in 4½ hours we did just over 4 miles. We are 16 from our depot. If we only find the correct proportion of food there and this surface continues, we may get to the next depot [Mt Hooper, 72 miles farther] but not to One Ton Camp. We hope against hope that the dogs have been to Mt Hooper; then we might pull through. If there is a shortage of oil again we can have little hope. One feels that for poor Oates the crisis is near, but none of us are improving, though we are wonderfully fit considering the really excessive work we are doing. We are only kept going by good food. No wind this morning till a chill northerly air came ahead. Sun bright and cairns showing up well. I should like to keep the track to the end.

Thursday, 8 March—Lunch. Worse and worse in morning; poor Oates's left foot can never last out, and time over foot gear something awful. Have to wait in night foot gear for nearly an hour before I start changing, and then am generally first to be ready. Wilson's feet giving trouble now, but this mainly because he gives so much help to others. We did 4½ miles this morning and are now 8½ miles from the depot—a ridiculously small distance to feel in difficulties, yet on this surface we know we cannot equal half our old marches, and that for that effort we expend nearly double the energy. The great question is, What shall we find at the depot? If the dogs have visited it we may get along a good distance, but if there is another short allowance of fuel, God help us indeed. We are in a very bad way, I fear, in any case.

Saturday, 10 March—Things steadily downhill. Oates's foot worse. He has rare pluck and must know that he can never get through. He asked Wilson if he had a chance this morning, and of course Bill had to say he didn't know. In point of fact he has none. Apart from him, if he went under now, I doubt whether we could get through. With great care we might have a dog's chance, but no more. The weather conditions are awful, and our gear gets steadily more icy and difficult to manage. At the same time of course poor Titus is the greatest handicap. He keeps us waiting in the morning until we have partly lost the warming effect of our good breakfast, when the only wise policy is to be up and away at once; again at lunch. Poor chap! it is too pathetic to watch him; one cannot but try to cheer him up.

Yesterday we marched up the depot, Mt Hooper. Cold comfort. Shortage on our allowance all round. I don't know that anyone is to blame. The dogs which would have been our salvation have evidently failed. Meares had a bad trip home I suppose.

This morning it was calm when we breakfasted, but the wind came from the WNW as we broke camp. It rapidly grew in strength. After travelling for half an hour I saw that none of us could go on facing such conditions. We were forced to camp and are spending the rest of the day in a comfortless blizzard camp, wind quite foul.

Sunday, 11 March—Titus Oates is very near the end, one feels. What we or he will do, God only knows. We discussed the matter after breakfast; he is a brave fine fellow and understands the situation, but he practically asked for advice. Nothing could be said but to urge him to march as long as he could. One satisfactory result to the discussion; I practically ordered Wilson to hand over the means of ending our troubles to us, so that any one of us may know how to do so. Wilson had no choice between doing so and our ransacking the medicine case. We have 30 opium tabloids apiece and he is left with a tube of morphine. So far the tragical side of our story.

The sky completely overcast when we started this morning. We could see nothing, lost the tracks, and doubtless have been swaying a good deal since— 3·1 miles for the forenoon—terribly heavy dragging —expected it. Know that 6 miles is about the limit of our endurance now, if we get no help from wind or surfaces. We have 7 days' food and should be about 55 miles from One Ton Camp tonight, $6 \times 7 = 42$, leaving us 13 miles short of our distance, even if things get no worse. Meanwhile the season rapidly advances.

Monday, 12 March—We did 6·9 miles yesterday, under our necessary average. Things are left much the same, Oates not pulling much, and now with

hands as well as feet pretty well useless. We did
4 miles this morning in 4 hours 20 minutes—we
may hope for 3 this afternoon, $7 \times 6 = 42$. We shall
be 47 miles from the depot. I doubt if we can
possibly do it. The surface remains awful, the cold
intense, and our physical condition running down.
God help us! Not a breath of favourable wind for
more than a week, and apparently liable to head
winds at any moment.

Wednesday, 14 March—No doubt about the going
downhill, but everything going wrong for us.
Yesterday we woke to a strong northerly wind with
temp. $-37°$. Couldn't face it, so remained in camp
till 2, then did $5\frac{1}{4}$ miles. Wanted to march later, but
party feeling the cold badly as the breeze (N) never
took off entirely, and as the sun sank the temp. fell.
Long time getting supper in dark.

This morning started with southerly breeze, set
sail and passed another cairn at good speed; half-
way, however, the wind shifted to W by S or WSW,
blew through our wind clothes and into our mits.
Poor Wilson horribly cold, could not get off ski for
some time. Bowers and I practically made camp,
and when we got into the tent at last we were all
deadly cold. Then temp. now midday down $-43°$
and the wind strong. We *must* go on, but now the
making of every camp must be more difficult and
dangerous. It must be near the end, but a pretty
merciful end. Poor Oates got it again in the foot. I
shudder to think what it will be like tomorrow. It is
only with greatest pains rest of us keep off frostbites.
No idea there could be temperatures like this at this
time of year with such winds. Truly awful outside
the tent. Must fight it out to the last biscuit, but
can't reduce rations.

Friday, 16 March or Saturday, 17—Lost track of
dates, but think the last correct. Tragedy all along
the line. At lunch, the day before yesterday, poor
Titus Oates said he couldn't go on; he proposed we
should leave him in his sleeping-bag. That we could
not do, and we induced him to come on, on the
afternoon march. In spite of its awful nature for him
he struggled on and we made a few miles. At night
he was worse and we knew the end had come.

Should this be found I want these facts recorded.
Oates's last thoughts were of his mother, but
immediately before he took pride in thinking that
his regiment would be pleased with the bold way in
which he met his death. We can testify to his
bravery. He has borne intense suffering for weeks
without complaint, and to the very last was able and
willing to discuss outside subjects. He did not—
would not—give up hope till the very end. He was
a brave soul. This was the end. He slept through
the night before last, hoping not to wake; but he
woke in the morning—yesterday. It was blowing a
blizzard. He said, 'I am just going outside and may
be some time.' He went out into the blizzard and
we have not seen him since.

I take this opportunity of saying that we have
stuck to our sick companions to the last. In case of
Edgar Evans, when absolutely out of food and he
lay insensible, the safety of the remainder seemed to
demand his abandonment, but Providence mercifully
removed him at this critical moment. He died a
natural death, and we did not leave him till two
hours after his death. We knew that poor Oates was
walking to his death, but though we tried to
dissuade him, we knew it was the act of a brave
man and an English gentleman. We all hope to
meet the end with a similar spirit, and assuredly the
end is not far.

I can only write at lunch and then only
occasionally. The cold is intense, $-40°$ at midday.
My companions are unendingly cheerful, but we are
all on the verge of serious frostbites, and though we
constantly talk of fetching through I don't think any
one of us believes it in his heart.

We are cold on the march now, and at all times
except meals. Yesterday we had to lay up for a
blizzard and today we move dreadfully slowly. We
are at No. 14 pony camp, only two pony marches
from One Ton Depot. We leave here our theodolite,
a camera, and Oates's sleeping-bags. Diaries, etc.,
and geological specimens carried at Wilson's special
request, will be found with us or on our sledge.

Sunday, 18 March—Today, lunch, we are 21 miles
from the depot. Ill fortune presses, but better may
come. We have had more wind and drift from ahead
yesterday; had to stop marching; wind NW, force 4,
temp. $-35°$. No human being could face it, and we
are worn out *nearly*.

My right foot has gone, nearly all the toes—two
days ago I was proud possessor of best feet. These
are the steps of my downfall. Like an ass I mixed a
small spoonful of curry powder with my melted
pemmican—it gave me violent indigestion. I lay
awake and in pain all night; woke and felt done on
the march; foot went and I didn't know it. A very
small measure of neglect and have a foot which is
not pleasant to contemplate. Bowers takes first place
in condition, but there is not much to choose after
all. The others are still confident of getting through
—or pretend to be—I don't know! We have the
last *half* fill of oil in our primus and a very small
quantity of spirit—this alone between us and thirst.
The wind is fair for the moment, and that is
perhaps a fact to help. The mileage would have

We shall stick it out
to the end but we
are getting weaker of
course and the end
cannot be far

It seems a pity, but
I do not think I can
write more —
                    R Scott

Last Entry

For Gods Sake look
after our people

seemed ridiculously small on our outward journey.

Monday, 19 March—Lunch. We camped with difficulty last night, and were dreadfully cold till after our supper of cold pemmican and biscuit and a half a pannikin of cocoa cooked over the spirit. Then, contrary to expectation, we got warm and all slept well. Today we started in the usual dragging manner. Sledge dreadfully heavy. We are 15½ miles from the depot and ought to get there in three days. What progress! We have two days' food but barely a day's fuel. All our feet are getting bad—Wilson's best, my right foot worst, left all right. There is no chance to nurse one's feet till we can get hot food into us. Amputation is the least I can hope for now, but will the trouble spread? That is the serious question. The weather doesn't give us a chance—the wind from N to NW and −40° temp. today.

Wednesday, 21 March—Got within 11 miles of depot Monday night;* had to lay up all yesterday in severe blizzard. Today forlorn hope, Wilson and Bowers going to depot for fuel.

Thursday, 22 and 23 March—Blizzard bad as ever—Wilson and Bowers unable to start—tomorrow last chance—no fuel and only one or two of food left—must be near the end. Have decided it shall be natural—we shall march for the depot with or without our effects and die in our tracks.

Thursday, 29 March—Since the 21st we have had a continuous gale from WSW and SW. We had fuel to make two cups of tea apiece and bare food for two days on the 20th. Every day we have been ready to start for our depot *11 miles* away, but outside the door of the tent it remains a scene of whirling drift. I do not think we can hope for any better things now. We shall stick it out to the end, but we are getting weaker, of course, and the end cannot be far.

It seems a pity, but I do not think I can write more.

R. SCOTT

Last entry.

For God's sake look after our people.

Eight months later, in November 1912, after winter had passed, the tent was discovered by a search party from the hut under Atkinson, who wrote, 'It was an object partially snowed up and looking like a cairn. Before it were the ski sticks and in front of them a bamboo which probably was the mast of the sledge . . . Inside the tent were the bodies of Captain Scott, Doctor Wilson and Lieutenant Bowers. Wilson and Bowers were found in the attitude of sleep, their sleeping-bags closed over their heads as

* The 60th camp from the Pole.

they would naturally close them. Scott died later. He had thrown back the flaps of his sleeping-bag and opened his coat. The little wallet containing the three notebooks was under his shoulders and his arm flung across Wilson. They had pitched their tent well and it had withstood all the blizzards of an exceptionally hard winter.'

Scott had written many private letters and a *Message to the Public* explaining the causes of the disaster:

MESSAGE TO THE PUBLIC

The causes of the disaster are not due to faulty organization, but to misfortune in all risks which had to be undertaken.

1. The loss of pony transport in March 1911 obliged me to start later than I had intended, and obliged the limits of stuff transported to be narrowed.

2. The weather throughout the outward journey, and especially the long gale in 83°S, stopped us.

3. The soft snow in lower reaches of glacier again reduced pace.

We fought these untoward events with a will and conquered, but it cut into our provision reserve.

Every detail of our food supplies, clothing and depots made on the interior ice-sheet and over that long stretch of 700 miles to the Pole and back, worked out to perfection. The advance party would have returned to the glacier in fine form and with surplus of food, but for the astonishing failure of the man whom we had least expected to fail. Edgar Evans was thought the strongest man of the party.

The Beardmore Glacier is not difficult in fine weather, but on our return we did not get a single completely fine day; this with a sick companion enormously increased our anxieties.

As I have said elsewhere, we got into frightfully rough ice and Edgar Evans received a concussion of the brain—he died a natural death, but left us a shaken party with the season unduly advanced.

But all the facts above enumerated were as nothing to the surprise which awaited us on the Barrier. I maintain that our arrangements for returning were quite adequate, and that no one in the world would have expected the temperatures and surfaces which we encountered at this time of the year. On the summit in lat. 85°/86° we had −20°, −30°. On the Barrier in lat. 82°, 10,000 feet lower, we had −30° in the day, −47° at night pretty regularly, with continuous head wind during our day marches. It is clear that these circumstances come on very suddenly, and our wreck is certainly due to this sudden advent of severe weather, which does not seem to have any satisfactory cause. I do not think human beings ever came through such a month as we have come through, and we should have got through in spite of the weather but for the sickening of a second companion, Captain Oates, and a shortage of fuel in our depots for which I cannot account, and finally, but for the storm which has fallen on us within 11 miles of the depot at which we hoped to secure our final supplies. Surely misfortune could scarcely have exceeded this last blow. We arrived within 11 miles of our old One Ton Camp with fuel for one last meal and food for two days. For four days we have been unable to leave the tent—the gale howling about us. We are weak, writing is difficult, but for my own sake I do not regret this journey, which has shown that Englishmen can endure hardships, help one another, and meet death with as great a fortitude as ever in the past. We took risks, we knew we took them; things have come out against us, and therefore we have no cause for complaint, but bow to the will of Providence, determined still to do our best to the last. But if we have been willing to give our lives to this enterprise, which is for the honour of our country, I appeal to our countrymen to see that those who depend on us are properly cared for.

Had we lived, I should have had a tale to tell of the hardihood, endurance, and courage of my companions which would have stirred the heart of every Englishman. These rough notes and our dead bodies must tell the tale, but surely, surely, a great rich country like ours will see that those who are dependent on us are properly provided for.

R. SCOTT

The search party erected a mighty cairn, surmounted by a cross made of skis. 'There alone in their greatness they will be without change or bodily decay, with the most fitting tomb in the world above them' (Atkinson).

The following January, when the *Terra Nova* returned to take the survivors of the expedition home, a cross of Australian jarrah wood was erected on the summit of Observation Hill, overlooking the Great Ice Barrier and in full view of the *Discovery* winter quarters. On it were inscribed the names of Scott, Wilson, Oates, Bowers and Evans and this line from Tennyson's *Ulysses*:

To strive, to seek, to find and not to yield.

The cross stands there still.

Bibliography and acknowledgements

Amundsen, Roald
The South Pole: an account of the Norwegian Antarctic expedition in the "Fram" 1910–12, translated from the Norwegian by A. G. Chater, 2 vols, London, 1912

Arnold, H. J. P.
Photographer of the World: the biography of Herbert Ponting, London, Hutchinson, 1969

Bernacchi, L. C.
A very gallant gentleman, London, 1933

Cherry-Garrard, Apsley
The Worst Journey in the World: Antarctic 1910–13, London, 1922

Debenham, Frank
In the Antarctic: stories of Scott's 'last expedition', London, 1952

Evans, Edward R. G. R.
South with Scott, London, 1921

Gwynn, Stephen
Captain Scott, London, 1929

Kennet, Kathleen, *Lady*
Self-portrait of an Artist [Lady Scott], London, 1949

Lashly, William
Under Scott's command, London, 1969

Ludlam, Harry
Captain Scott, the full story, London, 1965

Ponting, Herbert G.,
In Lotus-land Japan, London, 1910
The Great White South, London, 1921

Pound, Reginald
Scott of the Antarctic, London, 1966

Priestley, Raymond E.
Antarctic Adventure: Scott's northern party, London, 1914 (being reprinted)

Scott, Robert Falcon
The Voyage of the 'Discovery', London, 1905
Scott's Last Expedition, vols 1 and 2, arranged by L. Huxley, London, 1913

Seaver, George
'Birdie' Bowers of the Antarctic, London, 1938
Edward Wilson of the Antarctic, London, 1933 (paperback, 1966)
Edward Wilson, Nature Lover, London, 1937
The Faith of Edward Wilson, London, 1948
Scott of the Antarctic, London, 1940

South Polar Times, vol. 3
London, 1914

Taylor, Thomas Griffith
With Scott: the silver lining, London, 1916

Wilson, Edward Adrian
Birds of the Antarctic, edited by Brian Roberts, London, 1967
Diary of the 'Terra Nova' expedition to the Antarctic 1910–32, London, 1972

Acknowledgements
All photographs in this book are reproduced by kind permission of Paul Popper Ltd.
We are grateful to the following publishers and bodies for permission to reproduce extracts from the books listed below:
The Scott Polar Research Institute and Blandford Press Ltd for E. A. Wilson's *Diary of the Terra Nova Expedition to the Antarctic, 1910–12;* J. M. Dent & Sons Ltd for Herbert Ponting's *In Lotus-land Japan;* Duckworth and Co. Ltd for Herbert Ponting's *The Great White South;* the Bodley Head Ltd for Gwynn's Preface to *Scott's Last Expedition.*